CALIFORNIA BISTRO

MENUS FOR ENTERTAINING

· · · · · · · ·

TONY Di LEMBO

CB
CONTEMPORARY
BOOKS
CHICAGO

Library of Congress Cataloging-in-Publication Data

Di Lembo, Tony.
    California bistro : menus for entertaining / Tony di Lembo.
        p.   cm.
    Includes index.
    ISBN 0-8092-3979-5 (pbk.)
    1. Cookery, American—California style.   2. Entertaining.
3. Menus.   I. Title.
TX715.2.C34D5   1991
641.59794—dc20   91-5042
                                                            CIP

Published by Contemporary Books, Inc.
180 North Michigan Avenue, Chicago, Illinois 60601
Manufactured in the United States of America
International Standard Book Number: 0-8092-3979-5

To the memory of my grandmother, Til,
whose cooking has always inspired me.
And to Mom and Dad,
who were always there when times were tough.

CONTENTS

SPRING

· · · · · · · ·

SALMON RUN

APRIL VIOLETS

A LAMB'S TALE

Springtime Luncheon

Chilled Cucumber Soup with Dill Pesto 30

Jumbo Shrimp and Asparagus Tips Tossed with
Saffron Fusilli, Chopped Tomato, and Slivered Garlic 31

Papaya and Mango with Honey Lime Dressing 32

Rainy Nights

Wonton Ravioli Stuffed with Roasted Eggplant
and Goat Cheese Sautéed in Fresh Tomato and Oregano 33

Baby Lettuces with Champagne Vinaigrette 34

Ricotta Cheesecake and Marsala Wine Cream 35

Summer
· · · · · · ·

The Griller

Spinach Salad with Orange Mustard Vinaigrette 38

Charred Garlicky Skirt Steaks 39

Red Onion Relish 40

Grilled Tomatoes and Rosemary Potatoes 40

Fresh Blueberry Cobbler with Cinnamon Ice Cream 41

La Fiesta

Guacamole and Corn Tortilla Chips 43

Chicken Enchilada Torta with Chili-Roasted Mole Sauce 44

Summer Vegetables with Lime Vinaigrette 45

Vanilla Caramel Flan and Fresh Berries 46

Backyard Barbecue

Roasted Eggplant and Red Onion Salad 48

Chilled Lemon Pasta with Summer Zucchini, Tomato, and Fresh Basil 49

Barbecued Free-Range Chicken and Baby Back Ribs
with Secret Killer Barbecue Sauce 50

Pasadena Nectarine Pie 51

The Picnic

Crusty Herb Bread and Kalamata Olive Tapenade 53

Roasted Red Peppers with Slivered Garlic and Basil 56

San Domenico Chicken Liver Pâté 57

Grandma's Dill Pickles 58

Walnut Fried Chicken Drumettes with Roquefort Yogurt Dressing 59

Italian Almond Biscotti 60

Cocoa Pepper Cookies 61

Autumn

....

Harvest Moon

A Chardonnay Taster

Octoberfeast

Afternoon Stew

Indian Summer

Winter

....

A Cozy Winter Gathering

Super Bowl Sunday

PREFACE

As far back as I can remember, I have been surrounded by family and friends who share my passion for cooking and eating wonderful foods. When I was a boy, the first words I'd hear my mother speak every morning had to do with dinner that night. My father owned a restaurant, and when he was not working, his hobby became his vocation as he spent countless hours thinking and talking about recipes. When evening arrived, my mother prepared a meal from her heart, inspired by her inherent love for cooking and enjoying only the very best. Almost everything was made from scratch—herb breads, fresh soups, kitchen-canned tomatoes for sauces and pizzas, homemade garlicky sausages and pastas, dill pickles, fruit preserves, cakes, and pies. While my school friends talked about SpaghettiOs and Chef Boyardee, my mother was preparing homemade pastas and sauces. It was about then that I realized something unique was occurring in my family.

· · · · · · · ·

My mother's parents, Til and Matteo, were farmers, and most often their meals were products of their own farm, whether it was fresh-picked vegetables or a catch of freshwater bass, filleted by my grandfather and then handed to Grandma, who in turn would quick-fry them with a clove of garlic and a sprig of fresh thyme. My boyhood summers were spent on their Pennsylvania farm, and the activities of the day always centered around food. Breakfasts would include homemade sausages and farm eggs with slices of just-picked tomatoes and the oven-fresh crusty bread with Grandma's renowned (at least in their neighborhood) crab apple jelly. Later we would pick wild blueberries all afternoon, then sit and watch Grandma bake them into one of her succulent fruit pies. Sitting around the table and eating was always important, always special in my mother's family.

The other side of the family was no different. My paternal grandfather, Michael, made the wine. Each autumn the old wooden presses he brought from Italy were set up, and everyone would gather for the production, overseen by my grandfather. There was always plenty of food, especially Grandma Maria's homemade sausages, which she would air-cure through the cool autumn months and then preserve in olive oil and garlic for the rest of the year. Christmas Eve dinner was an event that took weeks to prepare. The pastas and raviolis were rolled and stuffed by hand. There was a special sausage made from pigs' ears and muzzles that would be stewed with tomatoes and garlic and served with mounds of pasta. It was a custom as old as anyone could remember, and it came to me from my great great grandparents, who farmed the Abruzzi mountains of Italy.

I can still recall Grandma Maria stirring great pots of polenta for exactly one hour. She would then pour the steaming concoction onto a large wooden board, spreading the top with her special tomato sauce and completing her work with mounds of grated Parmigiano-Reggiano cheese. The family would surround the table with forks in hand and eat off the board, drinking the strong red wine that grandfather poured with a vintner's pride. The dark roast coffee after the meal was always accompanied by Maria's lemon and anise pizzelle, thin waferlike cookies she made by squeezing a soft dough between the griddles of a hand-cast waffle iron that had been passed on to her by her mother. She stood at her small gas stove holding the iron over the flame, cooking one wafer at a time to perfection, timing the procedure by mumbling a short Ave Maria to herself since it was the perfect length.

And there I was in the middle of all this. As I began to realize that my affection and reverence for food went back many generations, I knew I had to become a chef.

. . . .

Nine years ago, I decided to attend professional culinary school, where I studied all the proper ways to handle foods, basic cooking techniques, food costing, and very boring, standardized recipes. When I graduated, I felt there was still much about food and cooking I wanted to learn. Twelve days later I went to Europe, where I was to spend two years working in restaurants in Italy and France, discovering the fine art of cooking.

While in Europe, I met many people who shared my excitement. One of my most vivid memories comes from the first restaurant at which I worked, San Domenico, located in a small town hidden in the Italian countryside near Bologna. The owner was a man of impeccable style who converted his childhood home into what many consider not only the finest restaurant in Italy but one of the best in the world. The dining rooms are filled with antiques, silver, and crystal. The wine cellar is literally one mile of small tunnels burrowed out of stone underneath the restaurant and displays the most comprehensive selection of European wines imaginable, both young and very, very old. But what makes San Domenico the most renowned restaurant in Italy is, of course, its food.

Supplies for the day were brought to the restaurant every morning. My first hour was spent preparing live chickens for service—not something I normally do, though I had lost my squeamishness years earlier while watching my grandfather perform the gruesome task. Later that morning a peasant farmer entered the kitchen with a large burlap sack over his shoulder and unloaded pounds and pounds of fresh white truffles. The aroma permeated the restaurant for a week, until we had finished scrubbing and preserving them for use through the year. The people who worked for San Domenico were from all over the world and were all there for the same purpose—to learn from each other and exchange customs and traditions through this grand restaurant.

········

Months later I traveled to the Mediterranean coastline and discovered another special place. Here a robust Chef Angelo operates a restaurant that bears his name, a place considered by many of the finest authorities on Italian cuisine to offer a landmark dining experience. The chef's knowledge of Italian food is extensive; his inspirations are earthy and always based on strict Italian tradition, reminiscent of my days with my grandmothers. And the freshness of everything can be sensed: Vegetables are picked and received daily, and the fresh herbs he uses are nurtured in the garden just outside his kitchen. The fish is still alive when it arrives at the restaurant. Most of the cooking is done on wood-burning grills, and all pastas are rolled and cut to order. Often Chef Angelo takes the pasta to the table still boiling in water and finishes preparing it by making a sauce at tableside. He taught me more than anyone about basic flavor combinations. I never stopped learning during the months I spent with him.

········

I had also been hearing of a restaurant in Milan since the first day I landed in Italy and had to see for myself what everyone was talking about. A small place, La Scaletta has a two-month waiting list; both local people and international celebrities keep the phone ringing in hopes of experiencing its delights. The kitchen walls are covered with autographed glossy prints of famous patrons as well as restaurant reviews and awards. The restaurant belongs to Signora Pina Bellini and her son, Aldo, who oversees the dining room while his mother works daily miracles in the kitchen.

Pina served her apprenticeship in France many years before when, as she told me, "it was unheard of for a woman to work in a professional kitchen—they didn't allow it." After her husband was killed in the war, she raised her infant son while working full-time in restaurants all over Italy. Now, 45 years later, she runs her own restaurant and performs for only 35 anointed people every evening. Her knowledge of cuisines, both classical and nouvelle, astonished me time and again. Her repertoire seemed endless, and she was always willing to share anything she could with a smile. Every plate combined tradition with novelty and passed Pina's personal inspection before being presented in the dining room. I could have spent years learning at her side.

What intrigued me most at these restaurants was that for the first time I was surrounded by professionals whose greatest joys came from preparing an exquisite dish and then, more important, experiencing the product. The conversation during a meal was always about what was on the table, just as it was when I was a boy. We'd talk about the balance of the herbs, or what a perfect accompaniment to the dish something else might have been, or a great wine, or how we could make something even better the next time. There was a true love for cooking, and we enjoyed every minute.

· · · · · · · ·

Returning to the States, I was soon forced to explore a new way of preparing food. I began cooking for Barbra Streisand, whose overwhelming concerns are to eat great-tasting foods and stay thin. Now I was faced with having to perform culinary legerdemain: cooking for a true gourmet who loved food while making sure she didn't gain an ounce. I relied on the freshness of ingredients or special cooking procedures or marinades to enhance the flavors of foods I was cooking, cutting back on butter and cream. As I discovered the endless supply of unique and superfresh ingredients that makes southern California a cook's paradise, I quickly took to the California way of cooking, a style that has passionately influenced my recipes. Two years ago I opened my own restaurant, Indigo, in Los Angeles. Indigo has given me the opportunity to use these fabulous California ingredients to put together a variety of light and refreshing menus daily, with something to offer everyone. The emphasis at Indigo is on large portions of light cuisine—lots of grilled fish and organic poultry, highly seasoned with everything except fat. The pastas I was accustomed to making in Europe are served too, but they're flavored with vegetables and fresh herbs instead of all that butter and cream traditional European cuisine dictates. Our bread, scented with rosemary, garlic, and onion, has been so popular it has prompted the recent opening of Breadworks, a large commercial bakery, located just up the street from Indigo.

· · · · · · · ·

This book started one day when I came across the old handwritten notes and cookbooks of my grandmother Til. The pages and pages of her forgotten little master-pieces inspired me to begin translating her creations for use by today's cooks. Many of the old recipes took it for granted that you knew how to prepare them, so no directions were given at all—merely the ingredients. I relied on memory to make them as well as she did. Grandma had an impeccable sense for flavor and seasoning, and I hope my attempts at measurement would meet with her approval. This entire collection of recipes has grown from decades of cooking experiments carried out by many generations—each execution incorporating slight changes until a recipe finally becomes something special. Go at it with a passion. Savor the rewards.

T.D.L.

ACKNOWLEDGMENTS

I have met so many people over the years whose talents have in some way or another influenced this book. It is with great joy that I can now thank at least a special few. First, and most important among them, is my family: my grandparents—Til, Amedeo, Maria, and Mike—who showed me in their own particular ways the pleasures of cooking and eating; my father, Sam, whose faith and direction throughout my life have been invaluable; and my mother, Elaine, who taught me more than anyone about cooking and who is still the best cook in the family.

Special heartfelt thanks must go to my friends and partners Karen Salk and Jay Fagnano, with whom I shared a dream and opened a restaurant two years ago, and who diligently watched the fort while I was in front of my computer; and to the rest of the gang who make both Indigo and Breadworks perform each day. I am particularly grateful to Linda Zimmerman, who helped me immensely when it was time to check the accuracy of the recipes, and who was always there to take my frantic phone calls as deadline approached; and to Robert Lakin, the best friend and critic anyone could ever wish for. I am further appreciative to those who shared specific recipes with me: Jackie Ravel-Knezevich, Lydia Shire, and, of course, Renata, Angelo, and Malek.

As for my recipes turning into a cookbook, thanks to Stanley Ralph Ross, who encouraged me from the outset; to Peter Miller, my hard-working agent, who pushed and pushed until it happened; to my editor, Linda Gray, who listened patiently and eased the quandaries of a first-time author; to my copyeditor, Christine Benton, who so meticulously picked through my manuscript; to Georgene Sainati and Kathy Petrauskas, for artistic inspirations; and to everyone else who helped make this book a reality.

INTRODUCTION

Since the era when dinner was a wild boar spit-roasted over glowing embers, man has strived to enhance the primal experience called eating. Foremost in your mind as you prepare a meal from beginning to end should be the idea that eating is an experience of the senses. Focusing your attention on each of the senses when cooking is essential to dazzling your guests.

· · · · · · · ·

Presentation is of utmost concern. As a meal is served, the table should come alive with aromatic, vividly colorful foods—the savory golden brown roasted chicken, vivid green snow peas sautéed with red pepper strips, creamy white bean soup, baby pink salmon, or a giant summer salad filled with bright greens, purple radicchio, white Belgian endive, cucumber slices, red onions, cherry tomatoes, and black olives, with a few tangerine-colored nasturtium blossoms scattered on top. Just looking at the salad triggers a culinary reaction in your body to prepare itself for the pleasure of eating. Aromas from a capon roasting with garlic and herbs, a steaming seafood stew, or fresh-baked crusty bread ripped open at the table will create the same sensory stimulation. It's organic, and we all have it in common. It's something over which we have no control. This is what you must appeal to when cooking.

One of my most memorable food experiences took place one summer afternoon in the Tuscan hills of central Italy. We came upon a small, rustic trattoria with an outdoor barbecue and a few wooden tables hidden under the shade of a giant olive tree. Almost within reaching distance were lush grapevines laden with succulent purple fruit that would soon be squeezed to produce another vintage of this family's personal Chianti, a sample of which the waiter generously poured as we sat. The aroma from the grill was not just that of wood smoke. It was smoke scented with bay leaves, rosemary branches, and unpeeled cloves of garlic tossed on the coals to flavor the foods as they cooked. Deciding what to order was not too difficult since only one entrée was served: a T-bone steak meticulously charred over the wood fire by a stout gentleman who seemed as though he had been in charge of the grill all his life. As he moved the steaks to our plates, he drizzled a fine line of the local olive oil on each and presented them to the waiter with pride. The first aroma I sensed was olive, followed quickly by the herb-scented steak. The taste was no disappointment. We ate and sipped the Chianti and ripped the crusty bread into what the Italians call the *scarpetta*, or "little shoe," to clean the precious juices from our plates. It was truly a celebration for our senses, appealing to each, stimulating them without reservation.

. . . .

Over the years I have come in contact with many cooks and chefs. Some were exceptional, others fair. What always seemed to set them apart from each other was their ability to season food properly with salt and pepper. It seems such a trivial point to sprinkle on the proper amount of these two standard seasonings, but so often, after a great deal of time has been spent on making a dish special—cutting the onions just right or making a perfect sauce—it is spoiled by either too much or too little seasoning. I have also come to realize that it is very difficult to teach someone how to season properly, simply because our palates are all different. Some are accustomed to heavily salted food; others love a lot of pepper. What I constantly try to convey is that well-prepared food must be well seasoned for an *average* palate. For those who want to add more salt or pepper, the option is available.

How much is the proper amount of salt and pepper? Simple—it's up to the cook and guests. A good cook should season food so it tastes good to those who are eating, and the only way to determine the proper amount is by tasting. So often in this book I was forced to specify an exact amount of an ingredient that is truly a variable, such as salt, pepper, basil, or garlic. If you like garlic, go ahead and add a clove or three more. I was constantly reminded that home cooks love to measure, so you will find measurements throughout, though according to the preferences of my taste buds. Perfect if you are cooking for me. For yourself, you must experiment. There should never be too much or too little of a good thing.

When I teach cooking classes, I love to see the reactions of the class as I add oil or butter to something. There is always at least one health watcher who gasps at the amounts, slight as they may be. Adding a piece of butter or a drizzle of olive oil to finish a risotto, for example, always brings a shudder from a few. To these people I say, no problem; use less or none if you wish, but remember—the final creation will simply not taste as good; it's the price you must pay. Not demeaning the importance of good health and nutrition, the recipes that follow are all measured in moderation, "medium-rare" as they say. You must feel comfortable and confident to hold back sometimes or add more salt or butter if need be. For these ingredients I have entered the proverbial "to taste" along with a measurement, giving you the freedom to cook and taste. Sometimes you cannot estimate or vary a cooking amount, such as eggs or sugar in a baked dessert. Many recipes, especially pastries and breads, require exact measurements to be successful. One less egg in a soufflé may be disastrous. If you don't see *to taste* in the ingredients, don't estimate.

· · · · · · · ·

The menus in this book offer a variety of meals for a variety of moods. Each one is a complete meal and usually requires substantial effort. Good cooking is not always a simple task, and some menus are quite elaborate. Some are designed for occasions, perhaps a party, that require days of planning. The recipes in the "Celebrations" chapter, for example, are intended to be prepared by two or more people, with the cooks helping to prepare part of the meal in their own homes, then assembling for the celebration. These large menus offer day-before suggestions, spreading the preparation over two or more days. Remember, the menus are suggestions—if the appetizer seems too time-consuming for a particular occasion, or the dessert has too many calories, eliminate it or freely prepare something else. Follow your mood when deciding what to prepare. It's all part of the enjoyment of the experience.

COMPOSING A MENU

One day some friends and I were talking about cooking. It seemed that the most difficult part of it all was deciding what to cook with what. So often a great recipe or idea was found, but the rest of the meal was bewildering.

When putting together a meal, you must first consider the mood. For some reason Mother Nature makes us crave foods that are in season, and certain foods become special since they come around only once a year. You'll need a place to start, a specific menu item that becomes a highlight in the dining experience. Perhaps you run across fresh truffles or find sweet summer red peppers at a good price. Use them as a focal point and build your meal around them. During spring, for example, when asparagus is at its best (usually evident by its abundance and low prices at the grocery store), prepare it as a feature, such as in an asparagus risotto. The weather should naturally help you choose—use the barbecue in the sun or simmer a stew on a cold winter's night.

. . . .

Understanding the principles of food colors is a most important aspect in putting together a meal. Foods fall into four basic color groups—green, yellow, white, and red. Almost everything falls somewhere within these color ranges, though some compromising is necessary—carrots are in the yellow category, grapes in the red, and so on. However, as a basic aid in choosing what to serve with what, it's a good place to begin. What goes on the plate—and, for that matter, the entire meal—should be color-coordinated, with as large a variety of colors as possible. Mother Nature again graciously helps us make this choice. For example, with a simple roast chicken, mashed potatoes would be a logical accompaniment. But what else could be made? Mashed potatoes are white. Other white vegetables include turnips, for example, which once pureed can be a welcome change from heavier potatoes, perfectly complementing the chicken. Or perhaps rice can be prepared, or buttered noodles. They will all give the entrée its "white starch" component. What else goes on the plate? Another color. Green broccoli or peas or orange carrots are possibilities—not white cauliflower or pearl onions. This color coordinating is useful whether you're preparing a large buffet set with bowls and platters of food or choosing which vegetables to put into your pasta salad. At the market, purchase the items you don't see all the time. Usually they change with the seasons, and the grocery store has a way of pointing them out to you either by showing their abundance or offering you a special price. Keep in mind the seasons and the feel in the air. Picture what the final plate of food will look like. Picture the colors and sense the textures.

· · · · · · · ·

A major consideration when composing your menu is the number of people you're cooking for. Sometimes menus can be as much work for two people as they would be for a large group of friends. I have always found three or four people the ideal number to cook for at home; things just seem to fit better in my pots and containers. It must be due to the fact that the cookware industry gears everything for a typical family of four. Because of the rate at which food cooks and the moisture that accumulates in the pan, certain menu items simply work better when made in certain quantities. A big pile of diced onions, for example, when cooked in a small pan turn out quite different from a spoonful or two tossed in a hot skillet. The size of the pan and the amount of heat you use are very important in cooking, and I refer to these factors throughout this book.

· · · · · · · ·

The number of courses you serve should vary with your enthusiasm. If you're making dinner for yourself and a friend after a long day's work, you should opt for a one-dish meal of dried pasta or maybe a risotto that's quick, convenient, and doesn't exceed your energy level. If you cook for recreation, as many of us do, try a more complicated menu when you have time to play. The experience must be positive for the food to be good. Classic French cuisine was originally developed to be served in courses, sometimes up to 20 of them, including sorbets and other "palate cleansers," appetizers, entrées, desserts, liquors, coffee, and even the final "smoke" course. They were served over hours, by roomfuls of hustling waiters and kitchens with scores of cooks who had very specific responsibilities. Duplicating these intricate menus at home is pretty much impossible. Though the modern refrigerator and freezer allow us to do a lot of preparation ahead of time, how many courses you plan to serve still will depend mainly on your available time. The more you have, the more courses you can prepare, so you can vary your dining experiences from a one-dish meal to an elaborate dinner party.

Timing too is important—you want to be sure that the peas are hot when the roast is carved. And this is another place where advance preparation can help. Doing some things ahead, with just a final fillip to be added at serving time, frees the cook from kitchen duty to be with the guests. My heart has always gone out to the frantic dinner party cook who nervously carves the chicken with sweat dripping from his or her forehead. With the proper amount of planning, you don't have to go through this kind of stress.

. . . .

The suggestions and directions in these recipes have been written for all those persons who pride themselves on serving extraordinary food. It may be just one unusual recipe that you are seeking, or it may be an entire menu that appeals to your desire to experiment and serve new dishes. Whatever your cooking inclinations may be, this book is arranged in menus for any occasion from which you can gather a host of ideas and inspirations. It is dedicated to you—to all of you who, like me, enjoy cooking and eating the best that nature's bounty provides.

FUNDAMENTALS
AND TECHNIQUES

The fundamentals must be mastered in all art forms, whether you practice the scales on an instrument or learn how to use a knife to cut an onion. Such skills come with time and practice and make the difference between average and exceptional results. In my cooking classes students often seem more interested in learning how to cut or roll something than anything else, which is why I tend to give elaborate explanations throughout this book. Experienced cooks often just glance at a recipe and cook something they are very happy with. Others require copious directions. The following are basic guidelines to fundamental information and techniques you may require when preparing these and other recipes.

BUTTER
· · · · · · · ·

Butter is the basic fat used in French and other cuisines, as well as in most pastries. In recent years we have discovered that it not only is the most fattening thing you can eat but also does a good job of pumping up the cholesterol level. So we now find ourselves cutting back and, depending on what we're making, favoring other fats, such as oil or vegetable shortening. I was raised on Italian food, which uses olive oil in practically everything, and there wasn't much room for butter, except in cookies and cakes. For this reason I still emphasize oil in almost all my recipes, except where butter is essential.

When you do use butter, use it for sweetness and creaminess, a tad stirred into a sauce or melted on vegetables. Remember, it's made from cream and has a special flavor all its own, certainly necessary for some recipes. Always purchase unsalted butter for the recipes. Salted butter should be reserved exclusively for spreading on bread, though many still think sweet butter tastes better. Using salted butter in cooking can significantly affect the dish; it could turn out salty. Add salt with the shaker, not with butter. In many cases the butter should be at room temperature; that is always noted when called for in recipes. Otherwise it may be chilled or frozen.

GARLIC
· · · · · · · ·

I first smelled garlic cooking in olive oil as an infant. It has always been part of my life and part of my cooking. My grandfather grew garlic for the entire family. In the autumn he would harvest the bulbs by pulling them from the ground and then braiding the stems into large garlic wreaths. They hung in the cold cellar for use throughout the year in almost everything we cooked. Now, at the restaurant, I find myself buying 80 or so pounds per week to enhance the foods by giving them flavor and depth. Fortunately I buy garlic already peeled; if not, I would need one employee alone for that loathsome task. Recently in some upscale grocery stores prepeeled garlic has become available, stored in airtight plastic containers. This is the best way to purchase it if you are like me and will pay anything not to peel. If you're more conservative, buy large fresh bulbs that seem plump and healthy. Break off the individual cloves and pop them open by laying the side of a kitchen knife or a cleaver on the clove and gently hitting the side of the blade with your fist. The cloves will pop free from their skins. They should be used immediately. Avoid preminced garlic commonly found in the grocery store; it's always disappointing.

The cooking method greatly affects the flavor of garlic. Raw garlic can be quite offensive. It's important to remember in recipes requiring sautéing that the garlic is cooked in oil just until it begins to take on color. This is especially true for pasta sauces as the flavor of raw garlic can be particularly displeasing. The key with garlic is cooking it slowly so it never burns and becomes bitter. Roasting the cloves whole in their skins produces a sweet puree that is served in many countries with hot, crusty peasant bread and a glass of strong red wine.

HERBS
· · · · · · · ·

The availability of fresh herbs alone makes it worthwhile to live in southern California. I use them in all my cooking, and you'll find them constantly in the recipes. It seems so peculiar to me that lettuce and parsley can be found in almost every market across America at any time of the year, but to find a bunch of fresh basil or rosemary is usually quite impossible, even in the summer, in many cities. It all comes down to supply and demand. If you can't buy it, the answer is to grow your own. Whether you use a small window box or decide to plow your backyard, fresh herbs always add a special dimension to flavor and aroma. If your space is limited, it is best to plant just one or two herbs, basil and rosemary being the best choices because these are the two with the greatest difference in flavor between fresh and dried. Most other herbs have more subtle variations, but something in the drying process of basil and rosemary effectively eliminates the special aromas characteristic of these herbs. If you simply must use dried herbs, remember to use less since drying an herb tends to concentrate its flavor. In most cases, use about half as much dried as fresh.

OLIVE OIL
· · · · · · ·

Olive oil was not invented, but was found, settled on the bottom of olive crates. Over many decades the process of making olive oil has evolved to an art, as with making wine, and the final quality of the oils varies greatly from label to label. I have purchased many olive oils and still gaze with indecision at the complicated selection now available in grocery and specialty stores. I'm convinced that olive oil simply must be tasted and smelled to determine whether it's good. Never purchase a large quantity of unknown oil, regardless of claims that it is extra-virgin, since label laws are not enforced in most countries that produce olive oil and you really don't know what you're ending up with. You'll find dozens of beautiful bottles and labels, with oils ranging in color from light yellow to dark olive green. Their prices also vary considerably, though you'll find if you shop in a reputable market you usually get what you pay for with items like olive oil, wine, and meats. Purchase a small bottle and try it at home. Smell the oil for its fruity olive scent and taste it to make sure it's not too bitter. Generally, the more prominent the taste and scent, the more "extra-virgin" you might consider the oil and the more suitable it will be in recipes that call for extra-virgin olive oil. When extra-virgin is not specified in a recipe, you should use regular olive oil, a less potent and less expensive version. Extra-virgin olive oil's fruity scent and flavor are lost considerably when heat is applied, similar to the Chinese sesame oils and other nut oils. It is best used as a flavor enhancer, not a cooking oil. Just a small drizzle, always added just before serving, can exhilarate pastas, vegetables, or grilled meats.

PREPARING SALADS AND VINAIGRETTES
· · · · · · ·

As seasons go by, we see a growing variety of lettuces and greens appear at the market. Using an assortment of these transforms a simple salad into something special. Base your lettuce and other salad ingredient choices on color, texture, and flavor. You may combine many different lettuces or perhaps focus your salad on one particular green, such as watercress or endive.

Once the salad green is in your kitchen, it is best if washed quickly, dried thoroughly, and placed immediately in the refrigerator. I have always preferred to do the washing in a clean kitchen sink, plugged and filled with cold water. Cut or tear the salad assortment into bite-size pieces and gently toss everything together in the water. Now comes the most important part of all—getting the water off the leaves. Nothing is quite as detrimental to salad greens as water. It prevents the leaves from getting crisp and dilutes a well-seasoned dressing. The most proficient method of removing water is with a salad spinner, a plastic basket designed for this purpose; it should be a part of your kitchen. Spin the greens dry and chill them, uncovered, in a colander (or right in the plastic spinner bowl), so the cool air can circulate through the leaves. After about a half hour or so the greens should be crisp and chilled, ready to be tossed with other ingredients and dressing.

Vinaigrettes intimidate many cooks, as they did me until I began working for Barbra Streisand. Salads were a part of every meal, and I constantly struggled for variety and invention. She had a small blender that held just a cup or so of liquid, and I found it ideal for blending a vinaigrette. After a while I realized how proficient I was becoming in concocting tasty salad dressings. I would add all sorts of ingredients, blending them all together and measuring with my taste buds rather than with measuring spoons.

The key is to follow a basic formula. When making vinaigrettes, you should always use three parts of oil to one part of vinegar. For the oil you may use more common oils, such as vegetable or olive, or try a more exotic oil, such as hazelnut or avocado. If you're cutting back on fat, substitute some fruit juice concentrate for half the oil. It will not only give salad dressing a natural sweetness but will also give it body, so it clings to the salad leaves. There are numerous vinegars from which you can choose, such as balsamic, champagne vinegar and other wine vinegars, fruit vinegars, rice vinegars, and even vinegars already flavored with herbs. Lemon juice may be used as part or all of the vinegar in your dressing, but it usually needs a bit of sugar to balance the tartness.

You may prepare a vinaigrette by simply combining the ingredients in a small bowl, stirring until the salt is dissolved. I prefer a small blender, because it can puree together anything you put into it, from garlic, shallots, ginger, or onion to fresh herbs such as basil, mint, or parsley. Remember always to include salt and pepper. Salad dressings and vinaigrettes should be well seasoned since just a small amount is used on the salad. Often they are better if made in advance, giving the flavors time to mellow. If you're using an oil because you like the flavor, such as extra-virgin olive oil, you may want to add a few drops of the pure oil to the salad before tossing; it helps make the flavor and scent of your special oil more prominent.

TOMATOES
· · · · · · · ·

The tomato that you pick in the backyard garden, allowed to ripen to a full tomato red, is the only tomato you should use. Obviously this is impractical for all of us, so we instead purchase at the market what American and Mexican farmers supply us with 365 days a year. This enormous demand for tomatoes has caused farmers to harvest them young, while still green, so the fruit can stand up to the handling and shipping necessary to get them on the shelves within days. Usually they're still green, or perhaps pink. This is how they are purchased, and unless you allow them to ripen for at least a day or two, you end up eating another lousy tomato. The ripening procedure is constantly occurring, even while you're deciding whether or not to buy green tomatoes, so you must plan ahead, knowing they will be fully ripe in a matter of days. If you cook often, you should always keep tomatoes around; they keep in the refrigerator for a week or so as they ripen. To hasten this process, keep them in a paper bag at room temperature until they feel soft to your fingertips. They won't necessarily turn tomato red like the backyard version; it depends on how green they were when picked.

To remove skins from ripe tomatoes, cut a small cross in the bottom with cuts 1 inch long and ¼ inch deep. Plunge them into boiling water and boil just until the skins are beginning to peel free, usually a matter of 15–30 seconds, depending again on how ripe they are. When the skins can be peeled back from the cuts you made, drain them immediately in a colander and rinse with cold water until cool. Slip the skins off and cut them in half around the "belly." Gently squeeze out the juice and seeds, reserving only the tomato pulp for use.

PASTA
· · · · · · · ·
FRESH PASTA

If one food has seen a resurgence more than any other during the past decade, it has to be fresh pasta. Though some of us were fortunate enough to receive great plates of it as children, fresh pasta for the most part is new and relatively untackled by American cooks. Making fresh pasta does not have to be a laborious experience, especially with the invention of pasta machines and food processors. It can be made in four basic ways, and depending on the shape and quantity you want, you choose the method.

The first method is how Grandma prepared it, by hand, slowly pushing the dough away, turning and folding, and repeating the procedure for at least 10 minutes. This is how I made pasta years ago, when no machine was around to help me. Unenviably, I worked up a little sweat and a rapid heartbeat by the time it was over. Grandma used to tell me in her Italian dialect that the warmth of your hands was good for the dough. Nowadays the warmth of the food processor blade does just fine for me. The food processor method, a detailed description of which follows, is certainly my preferred method, whether I'm cooking for two or ten.

Another method of kneading the dough is by using a dough hook on a powerful electric mixer. This is especially useful for making large quantities of dough, though it takes substantially more time than using a food processor and does not necessarily yield a better product. The last method for pasta preparation is the way it's done commercially, with powerful machines that force the dough through a cut die, then slice it off into the hundreds of small pasta shapes, such as penne, rotelle, rigatoni, tubetti, etc., and allow it to dry. Commercially these boxed pastas rarely contain egg, only flour and water, which is what you should use if you want to make dried pasta. These large machines have now been reduced to a home-sized version that kneads the ingredients, then reverses to force the dough into shapes—your only alternative if you want small, individually cut shapes. This extruding-type machine also prepares long pastas, such as spaghetti or fettuccine, though I'm convinced that they are inferior to what can be made quickly with a food processor and rolled out with a pasta machine. I always opt for the food processor, though the choice is ultimately yours.

Handmade Pasta Dough

Whether you are working with only your hands or with an electric machine, there is a basic ratio of ingredients you will need to make fresh pasta, shown in the following chart. It is most important to remember, however, that the precise quantity of ingredients you use will vary each time you prepare pasta. This is why it's impossible to give the exact quantity of water that will be necessary to attain a soft dough. Certain flours absorb different amounts of liquids and, depending on the proportion of semolina to flour you use, you may need no water or several spoons of water.

Semolina is a special flour used mainly for pasta preparation, that gives the pasta an extra-chewy texture and light yellow color. The dough can be made using only semolina, two full cups, and no white flour, though 100 percent semolina pasta dough does require extra kneading, extra water, and can also be quite costly. I find that using half semolina and half white flour is an ideal balance, and you'll probably always need a spoon or two of water, unless you're using extra-large eggs.

As a general rule, you will require *one egg per person* for fresh pasta, plus one more egg for the whole batch of pasta. Therefore, for two servings you'll need three eggs; for four servings, five eggs; and so on.

Once the dough is prepared, it must rest for one hour. This prevents the dough from ripping as you roll it out. You can also make the dough a day ahead of time, oil it and wrap it in plastic, and then store it in the refrigerator overnight. Bring it to room temperature before using it.

No. of People	White Flour	Semolina	Salt	Eggs	Olive Oil
2	1 cup	1 cup	½ teaspoon	3	2 teaspoons
3	1½ cups	1½ cups	¾ teaspoon	4	1 tablespoon
4	2 cups	2 cups	1 teaspoon	5	4 teaspoons
5	2½ cups	2½ cups	1¼ teaspoons	6	5 teaspoons
6	3 cups	3 cups	1½ teaspoons	7	2 tablespoons

1. On a work surface, mix flours together in a mound; sprinkle with salt. Make a well in the center with your fingertips. Lightly scramble eggs and oil with a fork. Pour eggs into well.

2. Begin to mix eggs with fingertips, continually "pulling in" more flour as you work. Try to form the pasta into a ball, adding water as necessary to attain a soft, pliable dough. Scrape the work surface with a metal scraper and rub your hands clean once the ball is together. Knead dough, dusting with additional flour if necessary, until dough is smooth, soft, and elastic. This should take about 10 minutes. If dough is too dry, add a small amount of water to attain a soft, pliable dough.

3. Oil ball of dough and wrap with plastic wrap. Always allow to rest for at least 1 hour before making anything.

Food Processor Pasta

My grandmothers never did accept the fact that a food processor makes pasta as good as the heel of your hand, and they're probably right. Yet in our modern times, when every moment is important, a fresh ball of pasta dough popped out of a food processor, formed in just seconds, is a welcome relief.

The only limitation of the food processor is its size. The ingredients must be able to whirl around freely, which means the standard model can hold only enough to make pasta for two people. You can, of course, always make the pasta in batches and then knead them all together. The most common problem I've seen among students is the tendency to make the dough too firm. It should be soft and pliable—you can always knead in a bit of extra flour by hand. As with all pasta dough, allow it to rest for one hour before further handling.

1. Measure all ingredients and place them in the food processor fitted with the metal blade. Add no water at this point.

2. Turn the food processor on. As the machine is running, a ball of dough should begin to form. Wait 10 seconds and stop the machine. Feel the dough. It should be wet enough to stick together but not tacky. If it seems too dry, replace the lid, turn on the machine, and add 1 teaspoon of water to help form a ball. If it seems too wet, put in a teaspoon or so of flour. The objective is to have a clean ball spinning around inside the machine. Don't add anything until you give your previous addition a chance to be kneaded in for a few seconds. This entire process should take no more than 60 seconds. The dough should be soft and stretchable.

Adding Fresh Herbs and Seasonings

If you want to make a fresh herb pasta, such as Parsley Linguine (see Index), you'll certainly want to use a food processor, since the whirling blades not only knead the dough but also mince anything else you add, whether it's the leaves from fresh basil, parsley, dill, spinach, or whatever else you come up with. The important thing to remember is that these fresh leaves contain liquid, and you'll probably have to compensate with a little extra flour to make a dough. Make certain that anything you add is completely dried after washing—no extra water.

You can also get fancy and add other flavorings such as carrot puree, tomato puree, beet puree, grated lemon zest, and so on, making a rainbow of different colors, and I mean *colors.* Once boiled and tossed with a sauce, these colored pastas pretty much all taste the same, though you can detect different herbs or something like lemon zest or ground fennel seeds, depending on how flavorful your sauce is. Again, it's important that you don't add too much extra liquid when adding vegetable purees, or you'll end up with so much flour that you'll find yourself cooking for a crowd. A good alternative to the fuss of cooking and preparing a fresh vegetable puree is to use baby food. It comes in many "colors," and you can eliminate a lot of drudgery for a couple of spoons of puree.

Rolling Dough with a Pasta Machine

Once the ball of pasta is prepared and allowed to rest for an hour, it's time to tackle the pasta rolling. After your first few episodes, it should become a painless task, far less frightening than cutting apart a chicken. You must purchase a pasta machine if you don't already have one. They are not too expensive and can be found in specialty shops and some department stores. Almost all of them are imported from Italy, and if they contain instructions, they're almost always in Italian. So, you're pretty much on your own.

Begin by clamping the machine to a tabletop or work surface; make sure it's secure. Set the machine on the widest setting, usually "number 1." Remove plastic from the ball of dough and slice off your first piece, about the size of a slice of bread, about 4 ounces. Cover remaining dough with a bowl. Flatten and stretch the slice of dough with your hands until it's no more than ¼ inch thick. Place the edge between the rollers of the machine and, holding it in place with one hand, turn the crank and allow the dough to feed through the rollers. Fold the dough in half, on top of itself, and roll through once again, placing the folded edge in the machine first. Now fold the dough over itself so you create a piece that is exactly as wide as your pasta machine, about 5 inches. Pat the 5-inch-wide piece of dough through the machine again to get a strip of pasta that's as wide as the machine. This is especially important if you're making stuffed pasta, such as ravioli, or hand-cut pasta shapes. As the dough is stretched thinner by the machine, it becomes constantly longer, not wider, so remember that the width you begin with is what you end up with.

Set the sheet of pasta aside and slice off another piece of dough. Repeat procedure until you have rolled all the dough on the first setting. You should not require any extra "dusting" flour; if you do, you have made the dough too moist. Set machine on the next setting, number 2, and roll the strips again by starting them off until they "catch," then turning the crank with one hand and pulling the strip of pasta out away from the machine as it's rolled. You don't have to continue to feed the strip into the machine; the rollers will pull it through.

Once all sheets have been extended, repeat this procedure with all dough until you are at the next-to-last setting. At this point, since all machines vary, you'll have to judge whether you should extend the pasta through a thinner setting. A good way to test is by cutting off a 2-inch piece of an extended sheet, setting the machine one increment thinner, and rolling a tester. You'll probably know immediately if it's too thin. The final result should be the thickness of a typical strand of fettuccine or linguine. You'll have to be the judge. If you're making a stuffed pasta, like ravioli, you should keep the pasta sheets thin since they will be doubled together, one for the bottom and one for the top.

· · · · · · · ·

At this point you must allow the dough to air-dry for a few minutes, for if you try running the moist sheets through the cutter attachments of your machine now, the individual strands of pasta may not separate. Generally, depending on how moist you made the dough and the temperature of your kitchen, the pasta sheets should be dried sufficiently after about 5 minutes. Flip them over at midpoint to air-dry the bottom side as well. If the sheets come out to be longer than an average strand of pasta, about 1½ feet, cut them in half.

To use the cutter attachment, slide it in place in the metal guides on the side of your machine, move the crank over, and cut off a 3-inch "tester" once again. Feed it into the cutter until it catches, then turn the crank. If the noodles do not freely separate, you need additional drying time. Lightly dust the pasta sheets with flour and cut the noodles, grasping the long strands with your free hand as they exit from the blades and gently gathering them into small "nests." Set the nests aside until time to boil.

· · · · · · · ·

At this point the nests may be covered with plastic wrap and refrigerated for a couple of days if necessary. The nests should never completely dry out, or else they will become fragile and are liable to crumble in your hands as you handle them. Keep them covered with plastic wrap until you drop them into boiling water. To freeze the nests, allow them to air-dry for 30 minutes, then carefully place them in a container, cover, and freeze. Sealed properly, they will keep indefinitely.

· · · · · · · ·

To cook fresh pasta, bring a large pot of water (about 4 quarts per pound of pasta) to a boil. Add 2–3 tablespoons of salt. Drop the pasta into the boiling water all at once. This is important since fresh pasta cooks so quickly; otherwise it will not cook evenly. Stir the pasta with a wooden spoon and cover the pot just to accelerate the water's return to boil. Be careful that it doesn't boil over. After just a minute or two, begin testing doneness by removing a strand and tasting it. Generally, the more moist the pasta, the more quickly it will cook. When the noodle is tender and cooked through, yet not soft and mushy, immediately drain the pasta in a strainer. Vigorously toss the strainer to remove excess water and immediately transfer the pasta to a serving bowl. Drizzle a little extra-virgin olive oil over the pasta and move the noodles so they are evenly moistened. Ladle sauce over the top, lifting the noodles to combine. Pasta that sits without a sauce will clump together. Sprinkle with grated cheese and serve.

········

DRIED PASTA

The cooks of southern Italy, more than anywhere else in the world, have mastered the art of making and preparing both fresh and dried pasta. There are several significant differences between the two, concerning both preparation and type of sauce. As mentioned earlier, the dried pasta commonly found in the grocery store is made with flour and water only—no eggs, no salt. The eggs in fresh pasta make it perishable. You must refrigerate it, or it will turn rancid in several days. If the pasta is made without egg, it can be air-dried and kept in a closed container at room temperature for quite some time. This feature is one of the main reasons dried pasta became so widely popular.

The variety of dried pastas available today is quite extensive. Many different companies make many different shapes, and the brands vary considerably. The best are those imported from Italy, such as De Cecco. I find that these imported pastas hold up much better after cooking and give you more leeway in timing to reach the proper al dente point. The domestic versions tend to become mushy, though I'm sure there are several brands worth their weight.

As far as shape goes, you may substitute any pasta shape for another in most recipes; however, there are unwritten Italian rules dictating which sauce best matches which cut. The small *righe*, or "grooves" on the sides of some dried shapes, such as some penne and rigatoni, tend to help a thin sauce cling to the pasta after it's prepared. If you've made a rich cream sauce, you should opt for smooth sides, no grooves, for a better result. Certain pastas naturally blend with a sauce, such as linguine with clam sauce. With others you have much more flexibility. If you must substitute one cut for another, try to use something as similar as possible.

········

To cook the dried pasta, you should boil as much water as you can, about 6 quarts for a pound of pasta. Then comes the big question: how much salt should be used? In my cooking classes, when I add salt to the pasta water there is usually a gasp from the crowd, since it's probably much more than most are accustomed to. The water should be as salty as the ocean, requiring up to ¼ cup for a big pot of water. Remember that dried pasta contains no salt and that you won't end up eating ¼ cup of salt since only a small amount of liquid is actually absorbed during the cooking. Those who add a pinch or two of salt to the water might as well not bother, since it can't be tasted in the end.

If you're cooking cut pasta, dump it into the boiling salted water. If you're cooking a long pasta, such as spaghetti or fettuccine, add the pasta, then press it gently into the boiling water, allowing the bottom to soften as you push in the top. Once the pasta has been added, it must continue to cook at a rolling boil. Stir it occasionally with a slotted spoon for small shapes and a carving fork or pasta server for strand-type pasta.

· · · · · · · ·

Now comes the next big question: when is it done? To Italians it's al dente, "to the bite," a feeling and texture they learn early in life. To others it must be tasted. After the pasta has boiled for a few minutes (unless it's a very quick-cooking kind of pasta, such as angel hair), begin to test by fishing out one piece and biting it. If it seems almost done, maybe requiring only an additional minute of cooking, remove it from the heat. It's very important not to overcook dried pasta. It should be extra-firm since you'll continue to cook it in its sauce after it's drained.

Drain the pasta in a colander and *do not rinse*. In all my years in Italy I never saw one Italian actually rinse pasta. It's just not done. Cooked pasta has a lot of starch that clings to its sides, which helps the sauce cling to the pasta. Rinsing the pasta forces it to absorb extra water and lose this natural thickener. The only exception is if you're making a chilled pasta salad, in which case the pasta should be rinsed quickly with cold water to stop its cooking, then immediately tossed with a little olive oil to prevent sticking.

· · · · · · · ·

At this point the pasta sauce should be in a saucepan large enough to contain the sauce and all the pasta; it should be warm on the stove top. Shake the colander well to remove all excess water and dump the pasta into the sauce. Turn the heat to medium and mix the pasta around, being careful not to tangle long strands too much. Add Parmesan cheese, a dab of butter, a drizzle of extra-virgin olive oil, and continue to stir, finishing the cooking of the pasta in the sauce. If it seems too dry, add some water; if it seems too wet, turn the heat up to evaporate some of the liquid. The pasta will also absorb liquid as it finishes cooking, so don't add it too quickly. This process should take only a couple of minutes. Taste a piece or a strand. When it's ready, turn off the heat, cover, and allow to sit for a minute, then serve on individual plates or family style, in a large bowl.

SPRING

The first balmy days of spring lure us outside to feel the warmth of the sun and watch the trees blossom. Of all the seasons, spring is probably the most written about, talked about, and sung about. It's the time when blades of wild grass sprout along the roadside, the desert bursts into bloom, and the fruits and vegetables that are in short supply the rest of the year begin to appear at the market.

SALMON RUN

········

Belgian Endive and Dandelion Greens with Cabernet Vinaigrette

Broiled King Salmon Fillet with Lemon-Cilantro Butter
and Cucumber and Tomato Salsa

Chili-Scented Baby Pink Potatoes

Strawberries and Mint Crème Fraîche

········

BELGIAN ENDIVE AND DANDELION GREENS WITH CABERNET VINAIGRETTE

As a child I was assigned "weed duty" in our backyard every spring, yanking out each young dandelion with the aid of a screwdriver. It was a job that had to be done early in the season since they toughen as they flower and go to seed. The sack of dandelion lettuces was passed to my mother, who removed their roots and washed the greens over and over again. Recently in grocery stores, I have seen these spring greens sold, but usually only the long-stemmed, leafy variety. My favorites are still the tiny hand-picked ones. To this salad I've added Belgian endive since this crisp white-leafed lettuce lends a special sweetness, balancing the tartness of the dandelions.

Serves 4

Approximately 1 pound dandelion greens,
  well washed
2 heads Belgian endive
1 small red onion
Cabernet Vinaigrette (recipe follows)

1. If you're using small hand-picked dandelions, trim them by cutting off the root. Cut large dandelions in half. Remove any flower buds. Wash greens until all traces of sand and dirt are gone. Spin dry in a salad spinner.

2. Cut heads of Belgian endive in half lengthwise. Lay flat on cut side and slice on the bias into ¼-inch slices. Wash well, spin dry, and combine with dandelions. Cut off ends of onion and peel. Cut in half through the root end. Lay flat on cutting board and slice very thin. Sprinkle over greens and chill until serving time. To serve, combine with a few spoons of the vinaigrette, to taste. Serve on chilled plates.

CABERNET VINAIGRETTE
Makes about ³⁄₄ cup

½ cup extra-virgin olive oil
1 tablespoon red wine vinegar
1 clove garlic, peeled and minced fine
¼ teaspoon freshly ground black pepper
3 tablespoons cabernet sauvignon
1 tablespoon seasoned rice wine vinegar
½ teaspoon salt
¼ teaspoon sugar

Mix all ingredients in a small bowl. The dressing is best if prepared a day in advance.

· · · · · · · ·

BROILED KING SALMON FILLET WITH LEMON-CILANTRO BUTTER AND CUCUMBER AND TOMATO SALSA

Salmon runs in the spring, and the wise fisherman knows full well that is when it is at its most delicious. Among the Pacific salmon alone there are about five varieties, all differing in size, flesh color, and richness. The very best, such as the Oregon king salmon, are those caught in northern waters. As summer approaches, the catch comes from Canada and then later from Arctic Alaska and Norway. Salmon can also be found in the Atlantic and Pacific oceans, though the color, as well as the price, varies greatly in these species. Choose firm, deep-red-colored fillets as fresh as possible. It's important to remove the "pin bones" from the salmon fillets before cooking. This is most easily accomplished with the use of needle-nose pliers or tweezers. With a light tug they are easily extracted, leaving a bone-free fillet. If fresh cilantro is unavailable where you live, you may substitute Italian (flat-leaf) parsley.

Serves 4

2 medium-size cucumbers
4 ripe Roma-style (plum) tomatoes
1 small red onion
2 small jalapeño chilies, minced, *or* 1 tablespoon minced green bell pepper
Juice of 2 lemons
3 tablespoons vegetable oil
Leaves from ½ bunch cilantro, chopped (about ¼ cup)

1 teaspoon salt or to taste
½ teaspoon freshly ground black pepper or to taste
¼ cup unsalted butter, softened
1 tablespoon finely chopped cilantro
2 cloves garlic, peeled and minced
1 tablespoon olive oil
4 boneless, skinless king salmon fillets, about 7–8 ounces each

19

1. Prepare salsa by peeling cucumbers, slicing in half lengthwise, and scraping out the seeds with a spoon. Slice cucumbers lengthwise into ¼-inch strips, gather and turn them, then slice again to create a ¼-inch dice. Place in a bowl. Dice tomatoes to ¼ inch as well; add to cucumber. Peel onion and dice to ¼ inch; combine with cucumber and tomato. Add chilies, juice of 1 lemon, vegetable oil, ¼ cup chopped cilantro, and salt and pepper to taste. Mix well and refrigerate until serving time.

2. In a small bowl, combine butter, juice of remaining lemon, 1 tablespoon chopped cilantro, and salt and pepper to taste. Mix well and set aside.

3. Preheat broiler until hot. Mix garlic and olive oil together and rub on salmon fillets; sprinkle them with salt and pepper to taste. Place on an oiled broiler pan and broil 2–4 inches from heat source for about 9 minutes, until cooked medium. Divide butter among tops of fillets and continue to broil just until butter begins to melt. Serve with a generous portion of salsa over the top.

. . . .

CHILI-SCENTED BABY PINK POTATOES

As potatoes mature in the ground, their sugar changes to starch. An old, starchy potato is the choice for baking or mashing, but for this recipe the smaller, firm and sweet new potatoes are the ideal selection.

Serves 4

2 pounds small red potatoes
Salt to taste
2 tablespoons unsalted butter
2 cloves garlic, peeled and minced
1 teaspoon chili powder (hot or mild)
¼ teaspoon ground cumin
¼ teaspoon paprika
¼ teaspoon cayenne pepper
Pinch of ground cinnamon
¼ cup water
Freshly ground black pepper to taste

1. Boil potatoes in salted water until tender when pierced with a fork, about 20 minutes. Drain and allow to cool until you can handle them. Cut them into quarters and set aside.

2. In a large skillet, melt butter over medium-low heat. Add garlic and seasonings. Cook for a moment, just until garlic begins to color, and immediately add water and

potatoes. Gently toss over low heat, sprinkling with salt and pepper to taste. When hot, transfer to serving bowl and serve. The potatoes can easily be reheated in the microwave.

· · · · · · · ·

STRAWBERRIES AND MINT CREME FRAICHE

April is strawberry month. Nowadays, what with hothouses and jet planes, we can enjoy them at almost any time, but April always has been their peak period. Crème fraîche is really nothing more than homemade sour cream. Making it yourself with raw or pasteurized cream gives it its delicate sour flavor. The ultrapasteurized cream, however, imparts a bitter aftertaste. It keeps for about two weeks in the refrigerator.

Serves 4 (about 2 cups)

1 cup heavy cream
1 cup loosely packed fresh mint leaves
½ cup sour cream
1 tablespoon sugar
2 pints fresh strawberries, completely ripe
   and red, hulled

1. Scald the cream and mint leaves together in a medium-size saucepan. Remove from heat and steep for 15 minutes. Strain the cream into a mixing bowl. In a small bowl, thin the sour cream with a little cream, then pour back into remaining cream. Whisk together and pour into a glass jar with a lid. Cover loosely and refrigerate.

2. The next day, mix with sugar. Serve with whole or sliced strawberries and a sprig of mint.

· · · · · · · ·

APRIL VIOLETS

· · · · · · · ·

Steamed Stuffed Artichokes

Roasted Lemon-Peppered Chicken

Sweet Carrot Puree

Raspberry Rhubarb Crisp

· · · · · · · ·

STEAMED STUFFED ARTICHOKES

This recipe is presented in honor of my mother, who first introduced me to this simple and savory preparation for artichokes. The big ones, stuffed plump, are a meal in themselves. You must remove the stems of the artichokes so they can stand upright when cooking, but don't throw them away. Peel them and place them on top of the artichokes as they cook. I always end up eating them before the artichokes are even served. Serve the artichokes as a first course or as a side dish with the roasted chicken and carrot puree.

Serves 4

5 cups day-old Italian bread cubes, with crust
4 cloves garlic
Leaves from 1 bunch Italian (flat-leaf)
  parsley (about 1 cup packed)
1 teaspoon salt

½ teaspoon freshly ground black pepper
3 tablespoons grated Parmesan cheese
⅓ cup olive oil
4 medium-size artichokes
½ lemon

1. Place bread cubes in a food processor and run machine until coarse crumbs about the size of peas are made. Place crumbs in a large bowl. Peel garlic and mince garlic and parsley together in processor. Add to crumbs and sprinkle with salt, pepper, and Parmesan cheese. Mix well with hands. Moisten evenly with olive oil and toss.

2. Slice 1 inch off top of each artichoke and rub immediately with cut lemon. Cut the tip off each artichoke leaf with scissors. Discard loose leaves at bottom. Cut off stems at base and peel the skin off stems with a knife; rub with lemon. Wash artichokes well and pound them upside down on counter to remove water and loosen leaves.

3. Pack each artichoke with stuffing, dividing it evenly, by stretching leaves apart and placing about a tablespoon of stuffing in each leaf, starting with the bottommost leaves and working toward the center. Push a big pinch of stuffing directly into the center. Arrange artichokes upright in a large steamer or on a rack in a pot and add water to steam. Cover.

4. Bring to a simmer and steam for 45 minutes or until a center leaf of artichoke can be pulled out easily. Be careful not to allow pot to boil dry; add water as necessary. When artichokes are cooked, carefully transfer to serving platter and serve.

· · · · · · · ·

ROASTED LEMON-PEPPERED CHICKEN

I first made these chickens on a rotisserie, which yielded a moist chicken with crisp skin. At home chickens are usually roasted. If carving a whole bird seems formidable to you, purchase chicken parts that are equivalent to one bird (two leg quarters, two breasts, and two wings) then roast pieces on a rack for about an hour. The skin should be brown and crispy. Feel free to use any combination of herbs you desire.

Serves 4

1 2½- to 3-pound chicken
2 lemons
2 tablespoons olive oil
4 cloves garlic, peeled and minced
2 teaspoons salt
½ teaspoon coarsely ground black pepper
½ teaspoon finely ground black pepper
2 sprigs fresh thyme *or* 2 teaspoons dried
2 sprigs fresh tarragon *or* 2 teaspoons
  dried
1 sprig fresh rosemary *or* 1 teaspoon dried
Additional olive oil, salt, and freshly
  ground black pepper to taste

1. Wash chicken and dry with paper towels. Squeeze lemons into a small bowl. Add olive oil, garlic, salt, pepper, and herbs. Stir well, then smooth over surface and cavity of chicken. Put the two squeezed lemons inside the cavity. Allow to marinate for 30 minutes at room temperature. (Note: You may marinate the chicken in the refrigerator overnight, but omit salt. Sprinkle with salt right before cooking. Never marinate for a long time with salt as it will extract juices.)

2. To roast: Preheat oven to 375°F. Place chicken breast up on a rack in a shallow roasting pan. Tuck wings under chicken. Tent with foil. Roast for about 1¼ hours, until juices from cavity of chicken are clear. (Meat thermometer should read 185°F.) Allow to rest for 15 minutes before carving, tented with foil.

3. Carve chicken by removing legs and thighs. Cut chicken in half through breast, removing breast and wings. Arrange on a serving platter. Scrape out the insides of the cooked lemons and add to pan juices. Add a few drops of olive oil and season with additional salt and pepper as necessary. Drain and discard fat from roasting pan and spoon remaining juices over chicken.

· · · · · · · ·

SWEET CARROT PUREE

Medical pundits have concluded that beta-carotene, found in the lowly carrot, is apparently good for almost everything that ails you. Carrots are very low in calories (if you don't add the sugar and butter), high in nutritional content, and their bright orange color will set off every main course.

Serves 4

2 pounds carrots
¼ cup unsalted butter
2 teaspoons sugar
½ teaspoon salt or to taste
¼ teaspoon freshly ground white pepper
    or to taste
Pinch of freshly grated nutmeg or to taste
Fresh chervil sprigs or chopped fresh
    parsley for garnish

1. Peel carrots and cut into large chunks. Steam until tender when pierced with a fork (8–10 minutes). Allow to cool slightly in steam basket or colander.

2. Puree carrots in food processor, adding butter to each batch. Put in a large bowl and season with sugar, salt, white pepper, and just a hint of nutmeg. Cover with plastic until serving time. Reheat in microwave or in a saucepan over medium heat. Garnish with chervil or chopped parsley.

· · · · · · · ·

RASPBERRY RHUBARB CRISP

Raspberries and rhubarb are a combination that is as delightful to the eyes as to the palate. This is an easy recipe to toss together at the last minute.

Serves 4

½ pound fresh rhubarb, cut into 1-inch
  slices (about 2 cups), leaves discarded
4 cups fresh raspberries (about 2 pints,
  picked over)
¾ cup granulated sugar
1 tablespoon fresh lemon juice
1 cup all-purpose flour
¾ cup firmly packed dark brown sugar
1 teaspoon ground cinnamon
½ teaspoon freshly grated nutmeg
½ cup (¼ pound) unsalted butter
½ cup quick-cooking oatmeal

1. Preheat oven to 375°F. Butter a deep 1½ quart baking dish. Toss fruit with granulated sugar and lemon juice and pour into prepared dish.

2. Mix flour, brown sugar, and spices in a bowl. Cut in butter with a fork or pastry blender until the mixture resembles coarse meal. Mix in oatmeal. Sprinkle over fruit. Bake for 35–40 minutes or until topping is nicely browned and filling is bubbly. Serve warm with ice cream or cream.

. . . .

A LAMB'S TALE

. . . .

Spring Spinach and Egg Soup

Herbed Leg of Lamb with Sweet Roasted Garlic

Sautéed Sugar Snap Peas

Cassata with Fresh Strawberry Puree

. . . .

SPRING SPINACH AND EGG SOUP

This soup, called *stracciatella* in Italy, is one of the most delicious, light soups ever devised. It is best eaten immediately, but you can prepare the broth and the spinach and egg mixture in advance, as the final preparation takes just minutes to complete.

Serves 6

1 pound fresh young spinach *or* 1 10-ounce bag cleaned spinach
1½ quarts homemade chicken broth (as in Grandma's Cappelletti Soup; see Index)
Pinch of freshly grated nutmeg
2 tablespoons unsalted butter

2 tablespoons extra-virgin olive oil
½ teaspoon salt or to taste
¼ teaspoon freshly ground black pepper or to taste
¼ cup grated Parmesan cheese
2 eggs, lightly beaten
Pinch of sugar

1. Prepare spinach by gathering the leaves together and slicing it into ¼ inch shreds. Wash several times; drain in a colander.

2. Bring chicken broth and nutmeg to a boil in a medium-size pot. Melt butter and olive oil in a medium-size skillet over medium heat. Add spinach greens and sauté for 3–4 minutes, until spinach is completely wilted. Add salt, pepper, and cheese. Remove from heat and add eggs, mixing well. Slowly pour spinach mixture into boiling broth, stirring with a spoon. Add sugar and simmer for a minute or 2. Serve hot.

. . . .

26

HERBED LEG OF LAMB WITH SWEET ROASTED GARLIC

The aroma of roast lamb is quite unlike that of any other meat, and it's something that can be found in every culture around the world. Lamb alone is a fine entrée, but with the addition of the herbs indicated and the ubiquitous garlic, this is a most succulent dish. Removing the bone or, better yet, having your butcher remove the bone before cooking will be helpful when carving time comes.

Serves 6

2 whole bulbs unpeeled garlic
1¼ cups olive oil
1 small bay leaf
3 sprigs fresh thyme
Salt to taste
¼ teaspoon sugar
1 tablespoon fresh rosemary leaves *or*
   2 teaspoons dried

1 tablespoon fresh thyme leaves *or*
   2 teaspoons dried
1 bay leaf
2 additional cloves garlic, peeled
Boneless leg of lamb, about 5 pounds
Freshly ground black pepper to taste

1. Preheat oven to 325°F. Cut bulbs of garlic in half, around belly. Place cut side down in a small baking dish. Add olive oil, small bay leaf, and thyme sprigs. Roast for about 30 minutes, until cloves are soft. Cool slightly. Squeeze garlic from skins into a blender. Remove leaves from thyme sprigs and set aside. Add ¼ teaspoon each salt and sugar and about 2 tablespoons of the oil to the blender. Puree garlic until smooth and transfer to a small bowl. Stir in thyme leaves from the sprigs.

2. Chop together the rosemary, 1 tablespoon thyme leaves, bay leaf, and additional garlic, along with a little salt, until very fine, almost pureed. Open boneless leg of lamb flat, outside down, and rub with herb mixture, reserving a small amount. Sprinkle lamb lightly with salt and pepper. Close meat up and tie with about seven lengths of kitchen twine. Begin tying at the center, then alternate ends. Coat outside of meat with olive oil and rub remaining herb mixture over it thoroughly. Lightly salt and pepper the roast. (Lamb may be refrigerated overnight at this point.)

3. Preheat oven to 375°F. Place meat in a baking dish and roast for about 1 hour, depending on thickness of meat rather than its weight. A thermometer stuck into the center of the roast should read 145°F for medium. Remove from oven, tent with foil, and allow to rest for 15 minutes before slicing. Serve with a dollop of warm roasted garlic and garnish with a small sprig of thyme.

· · · · · · · ·

SAUTEED SUGAR SNAP PEAS

This special pea, eaten pod and all, is in abundance in late spring when it is still small and tender. Clean the peas by snapping the stem and pulling off the string, as you would a bean. Once cooked, they retain their firmness and won't get soft while they wait to be eaten.

Serves 6

½ tablespoon unsalted butter
½ tablespoon extra-virgin olive oil
½ shallot, minced fine
1¼ pounds sugar snap peas, cleaned
¼ teaspoon sugar
Salt and freshly ground black pepper
    to taste

Melt butter and olive oil together in a large skillet over medium-high heat. When sizzling, add minced shallot, sauté for a minute, then add peas. Sprinkle with sugar and salt and pepper to taste. Toss often and cook quickly. Drizzle some water in to prevent browning. After a few minutes the peas should be cooked but still crisp.

· · · · · · · ·

CASSATA WITH FRESH STRAWBERRY PUREE

Of all the splendid desserts I was fortunate to savor in Europe, this one in particular remains foremost in my memory. A variation on the classical cassata, this elegant dessert takes some effort but can be made a week in advance. Its smooth, ice-creamy texture is perfectly complemented by the fruity Strawberry Puree.

Serves 12

1 pound sugar (2 cups)
1 tablespoon water
½ pound (1 cup) pine nuts
¼ pound (½ cup) shelled pistachios
¼ pound raisins
½ cup light rum
9 ounces (1 cup) candied fruit (not
    citron)

5 ounces (1¼ cups) shelled hazelnuts,
    lightly toasted
1 quart whipping cream
1 cup egg whites (about 8–10 eggs)
Strawberry Puree (recipe follows)

1. Combine ¼ cup of the sugar and the water in a small saucepan. Bring to a boil and add pine nuts. Stir constantly with a wooden spoon over medium-high heat until water evaporates and sugar becomes granular. Continue to stir until nuts begin to turn light golden. Do not allow sugar to caramelize. Immediately dump onto a metal baking sheet; break candied nuts apart as they cool.

2. Blanch pistachio nuts in boiling water for 1 minute. Drain and peel off skins. Plump raisins in ¼ cup rum and soak candied fruit in remaining ¼ cup. Remove any skins from hazelnuts. Whip cream until thick. Refrigerate.

3. Prepare meringue by combining egg whites and 14 ounces (1¾ cups) of the sugar in a medium saucepan. Heat slowly, stirring to dissolve the sugar, until mixture reaches 110°F, warm to your fingertips. Pour into a large mixing bowl and whip on high speed until thick and velvety. Fold into the meringue the pistachios, plumped raisins with their rum, candied pine nuts, hazelnuts, and candied fruit with its rum. Mix well. Fold in the whipped cream until thoroughly combined. Pour into one large mold or bundt pan or smaller individual pans and smooth over the top. Cover with plastic wrap and freeze.

4. To serve the dessert, dip sides of pan in hot water until the cassata is free and invert on a platter. Smooth sides and refreeze. When the cassata is solid, slice loaf with a sharp knife. Spoon Strawberry Puree onto plates and top each with a slice of cassata.

STRAWBERRY PUREE
Makes about 2 cups

2 pints fresh strawberries
2 tablespoons light corn syrup
Juice of ½ lemon
Sugar to taste
1–2 drops red food coloring (optional)

Hull strawberries and wash well. Puree berries in a food processor or blender along with corn syrup and lemon juice. Taste the puree; depending on the sweetness of the fruit, add sugar to taste. Stir in food coloring if desired. Store in refrigerator or freeze for future use.

. . . .

SPRINGTIME LUNCHEON

········

Chilled Cucumber Soup with Dill Pesto

*Jumbo Shrimp and Asparagus Tips Tossed with Saffron Fusilli,
Chopped Tomato, and Slivered Garlic*

Papaya and Mango with Honey Lime Dressing

········

CHILLED CUCUMBER SOUP WITH DILL PESTO

Toward the end of spring large crops of cucumbers are harvested in California and
also in Mexico. This soup is a refreshing way to use these vegetables to start a meal
and titillate the palate.

Serves 4

> 2 large cucumbers
> 4 scallions, white parts only
> 2 cups buttermilk
> 2 cups homemade chicken broth (as in
>   Grandma's Cappelletti Soup; see Index)
>   at room temperature
> ½ teaspoon salt or to taste
> 1 teaspoon sugar
> Dill Pesto (recipe follows)

Peel cucumbers, halve lengthwise, and remove seeds with a spoon. In a blender or
food processor, puree them together with scallions and buttermilk. Pour into a large
bowl and add remaining ingredients except pesto. Refrigerator for at least 2 hours
or overnight. Stir well before serving. Garnish with a spoonful of Dill Pesto on top.

DILL PESTO
Makes about ½ cup

2 bunches fresh dill
2 cloves garlic, peeled
½ teaspoon salt
½ teaspoon sugar
3 tablespoons extra-virgin olive oil
1 tablespoon pine nuts, preferably toasted
¼ teaspoon freshly ground black pepper
1 tablespoon water

In a small food chopper or blender, combine all ingredients until a paste is formed. Thin with water to spoonable consistency. May be frozen and defrosted.

. . . .

JUMBO SHRIMP AND ASPARAGUS TIPS TOSSED WITH SAFFRON FUSILLI, CHOPPED TOMATO, AND SLIVERED GARLIC

Shrimp come in many different sizes, some as large as lobsters. For this recipe I suggest the jumbo variety as the small ones often overcook in the sauce. Saffron is a small flower pistil that's hand-"plucked" from the center of individual flowers that, in many parts of the world, cover hillsides with a brilliant shade of orange. A little saffron goes a long way, thankfully, since it's very expensive. This recipe was devised at Indigo, and it's now one of the most requested entrées in our repertoire.

Serves 4

16 jumbo shrimp
1 bunch thin asparagus
¼ cup extra-virgin olive oil
4 cloves garlic, peeled and sliced thin
Small pinch of saffron (about ¼ teaspoon)
1 cup fish broth or bottled clam juice
3 Roma-style (plum) tomatoes, diced

1 bunch fresh basil, julienned (about ¼ cup packed)
¾ teaspoon salt or to taste
½ teaspoon freshly ground black pepper or to taste
3 tablespoons unsalted butter
1 pound dried fusilli or other pasta shape

1. Peel shrimp, leaving tail flipper on. Split them in half lengthwise, starting at large end, halfway down, thus butterflying the shrimp. Devein the shrimp. Cut asparagus into 1-inch pieces on the bias, discarding tough ends.

2. Pour olive oil into a very large skillet. Add garlic and cook slowly over medium-low heat until garlic is soft and tender, about 6 minutes; mash it lightly with a fork.

Turn heat to high and add shrimp and asparagus. Add saffron, broth, tomatoes, basil, salt, and pepper. Bring to a boil, cover skillet, and turn off heat, allowing saffron to steep and turn the mixture a bright yellow. Add butter. Shrimp should still be uncooked in the center.

3. Boil pasta in salted water as directed in "Dried Pasta" (see Index). Drain pasta and add to sauce, stirring over medium heat to allow the pasta to absorb some of the liquid and to finish cooking the shrimp. If it becomes too dry, add a bit more broth. Pour into serving dish with shrimp on top.

· · · · · · · ·

PAPAYA AND MANGO WITH HONEY LIME DRESSING

Papayas and mangoes become ripe and plentiful in the late spring. A chilled plate of these exotic fruits, with their subtle flowerlike flavors, makes a perfect ending to a light brunch. Since most papayas and mangoes come from Hawaii, the farther you are from this tropical island, the more difficult it will be to find the fruits. A good substitute is either pineapple or a mixed fruit salad, since the lime dressing is very versatile. Papayas and mangoes must be fully ripe and yield to gentle pressure before being eaten.

Serves 4

1 cup sour cream
2 tablespoons Rose's Lime Juice
3 tablespoons honey
2 papayas
2 mangoes
Grated lime zest for garnish

1. Prepare dressing by combining sour cream, Rose's Lime Juice, and honey with a whisk. Refrigerate.

2. Peel papayas with a paring knife and cut in half. Scoop out seeds, reserving a few to garnish the dish. Slice each half into four wedges. Peel the mangoes by scoring skin lengthwise in four to six places; pull off skin. Cut fleshy "cheeks" from each side of pit. Cut them into slices. Spoon dressing onto plate and arrange fruit on dressing. Garnish with lime zest and papaya seeds.

· · · · · · · ·

RAINY NIGHTS

· · · · · · · ·

*Wonton Ravioli Stuffed with Roasted Eggplant
and Goat Cheese Sautéed in Fresh Tomato and Oregano*

Baby Lettuces with Champagne Vinaigrette

Ricotta Cheesecake and Marsala Wine Cream

· · · · · · · ·

WONTON RAVIOLI STUFFED
WITH ROASTED EGGPLANT AND GOAT CHEESE
SAUTEED IN FRESH TOMATO AND OREGANO

Wonton wrappers differ from pasta in that they contain no egg and are dusted with cornstarch instead of flour to prevent sticking. They come precut into small squares and are ideal for making ravioli when you don't want to fuss with fresh pasta. Since most ravioli fillings are quick to prepare, you can enjoy a ravioli dinner in a fraction of the time using these special wrappers, and the final dish, though not identical to fresh pasta, is a wonderful and light alternative. Eggplant works well inside ravioli, and goat cheese adds a creamy richness to the filling. If you can't find goat cheese, you may substitute ricotta. The filling may be prepared in advance and refrigerated overnight.

Serves 4 (24 ravioli)

RAVIOLI
1 medium-size eggplant, peeled
⅓ cup extra-virgin olive oil
1 medium-size onion, peeled and diced
3 cloves garlic, peeled and minced
½ cup or more water
¼ pound Montrachet or other goat cheese
1 teaspoon dried oregano
3 eggs
1 cup fresh bread crumbs
Salt to taste
Freshly ground black pepper to taste
1 package wonton wrappers
¼ cup grated Parmesan cheese

SAUCE
¼ cup extra-virgin olive oil
4 cloves garlic, peeled and sliced thin
2 pounds ripe Roma-style (plum) tomatoes, diced
1 tablespoon chopped fresh oregano *or* 1 teaspoon dried
2 tablespoons unsalted butter
½ teaspoon salt or to taste
½ teaspoon freshly ground black pepper or to taste
½ teaspoon sugar or to taste

33

1. Cut eggplant into ½-inch cubes. Put ⅓ cup oil in a large skillet and sauté onion until it begins to color. Add garlic and mix. Add eggplant and toss. Pour in ½ cup water and cover pan to cook the eggplant until soft—about 10 minutes. Stir occasionally, adding water just to prevent scorching. Remove from heat and transfer to a bowl.

2. Add goat cheese and oregano to hot eggplant and mix well. Add two of the eggs and the bread crumbs. Season with salt and pepper and mix well. Chill.

3. Scramble remaining egg with 1 teaspoon water and a pinch of salt. Prepare ravioli by laying out six wonton wrappers. Paint each lightly with egg, then spoon a tablespoon-size ball of filling into center, cover with another square, and seal, pressing out air. Cut with a round, scalloped cookie cutter. Store on a kitchen towel until boiling time. Ravioli can be frozen flat, then stored in the freezer in a sealed container.

4. To serve, bring a large pot of salted water to a boil. Meanwhile, prepare sauce by heating ¼ cup olive oil in a large skillet. Add garlic and sauté over medium heat until tender; mash with a fork. Add tomatoes, oregano, butter, salt, pepper, and sugar. Simmer for several minutes. Drop ravioli into boiling water and cook for about 2–3 minutes. Water may not reboil. Do not overcook. If the ravioli are frozen, cook directly from the freezer for a longer period until tender. Remove the ravioli with a slotted spoon and transfer to a colander; drain well. Spoon some sauce onto a serving platter or plates, arrange the ravioli on top, and top with additional sauce. Sprinkle with Parmesan cheese before serving.

· · · · · · · ·

BABY LETTUCES WITH CHAMPAGNE VINAIGRETTE

In some places baby lettuces are produced in hothouses and sold regularly in markets. The list of names for individual kinds of lettuces goes on forever—just remember to select a variety of colors, shapes, and flavors, keeping in mind that the tender young lettuces are best when dressed with a subtle vinaigrette made from a special vinegar, such as apple cider, herb-scented, fruited, or others you may have come across.

Serves 4 (about ⅓ cup vinaigrette)

Approximately 1 pound assorted baby lettuces
¼ cup extra-virgin olive oil
2 tablespoons champagne vinegar
½ shallot, peeled and minced

¼ teaspoon dry mustard
¼ teaspoon salt or to taste
¼ teaspoon sugar or to taste
¼ teaspoon freshly ground black pepper or to taste

1. Wash lettuces well and trim any roots. Small heads may be left whole, or the leaves may be separated. Dry in a salad spinner and refrigerate until crisp.

2. Prepare vinaigrette by stirring all remaining ingredients together in a bowl until salt dissolves, making sure dressing is well seasoned. The vinaigrette is best if made the day before. Lightly toss the lettuce greens with the vinaigrette and arrange on chilled plates.

. . . .

RICOTTA CHEESECAKE AND MARSALA WINE CREAM

This cheesecake must be prepared the day before and allowed to set overnight. The crust is formed with a basic cookie dough. Any leftover dough may be frozen or baked into sugar cookies. The wine cream can be made ahead of time as well, but remember to whip it lightly before serving.

Makes 1 9-inch cheesecake, serving 12

PIECRUST DOUGH
½ cup sugar
½ cup (¼ pound) unsalted butter, softened
1 egg
1¼ cups all-purpose flour
1 teaspoon vanilla extract

RICOTTA CHEESE FILLING
4 cups ricotta cheese
4 eggs, separated
⅓ cup plus 1 tablespoon sugar
¼ teaspoon salt
1 tablespoon vanilla extract
2 tablespoons grated orange zest
½ teaspoon ground cinammon
¼ teaspoon freshly grated nutmeg
3 tablespoons all-purpose flour
¼ cup pine nuts, toasted
¼ cup candied fruit, wet with marsala
¼ cup raisins, soaked in marsala

MARSALA WINE CREAM
1 cup whipping cream
2 teaspoons sugar
½ teaspoon vanilla extract
¼ cup marsala

1. To make the dough, cream together sugar and butter until fluffy. Add egg and mix well. Add flour in three parts and vanilla extract and mix until just blended. Form into two balls and wrap with plastic wrap. Refrigerate until firm enough to roll.

2. Preheat oven to 450°F. Roll one ball out on a floured surface and trim to the size of the bottom of a 9-inch springform pan. Place pastry on bottom and bake for 5–6 minutes. Cool. Meanwhile, divide remaining dough into three parts. Roll each into a 2½-inch-wide strip. Place strips on the sides of the assembled pan and seal sides to bottom. Set aside.

3. Preheat the oven to 350°F. To make the filling, whip ricotta and add egg yolks, ⅓ cup sugar, salt, vanilla, orange zest, and spices. Sprinkle with the flour and mix. Fold in pine nuts, candied fruit, and raisins.

4. Whip egg whites with a tablespoon of sugar until thick. Fold egg whites into ricotta mixture and pour into springform pan. Bake for 45 minutes to 1 hour, until center is firm and filling is set. Allow to cool for several minutes, then loosen from sides of pan. Refrigerate overnight before cutting.

5. To make the wine cream, whip cream, sugar, and vanilla until thick. Mix in marsala to form a heavy cream. Refrigerate.

6. Ricotta pie is best if it sits at room temperature for about 30 minutes before being served. Serve with a couple of spoonfuls of wine cream. The pie keeps in the refrigerator for up to 1 week and also freezes well.

· · · · · · · ·

SUMMER

We look forward to summer all year, grumble once it's upon us, and rue the moment it's over. Nevertheless, millions of backyard chefs trot out the barbecue and charcoal to embark on a season of cooking outdoors. Truly this is the season for dining al fresco, especially on a warm, windswept evening.

THE GRILLER

Spinach Salad with Orange Mustard Vinaigrette

Charred Garlicky Skirt Steaks

Red Onion Relish

Grilled Tomatoes and Rosemary Potatoes

Fresh Blueberry Cobbler with Cinnamon Ice Cream

. . . .

SPINACH SALAD WITH ORANGE MUSTARD VINAIGRETTE

Take advantage of fresh spinach during early summer, when it is most abundant. This is one of the few salads that don't have to be ice-cold upon serving and are well suited to those balmy summer evenings. The vinaigrette uses orange juice concentrate for a zestful flavor and can be made days in advance. Add a few vine-ripened tomato wedges or even artichoke hearts if you'd like, and garnish the tops of individual salads with a little orange zest or some chopped walnuts.

Serves 4

1 pound young spinach leaves, stems removed and leaves torn up	1 tablespoon coarse-grained mustard
2 eggs	2 tablespoons frozen orange juice concentrate
¼ pound bacon	¼ cup Italian (flat-leaf) parsley leaves
1 medium-size red onion, peeled	¼ cup cider vinegar
½ cup olive oil	½ teaspoon salt
1 clove garlic	¼ teaspoon freshly ground black pepper

1. Wash the spinach leaves in several changes of cold water. Drain them and spin them dry in a salad spinner or toss with paper towels. Place in a large bowl and refrigerate.

2. Hard-cook the eggs in water for 10 minutes. After peeling, remove yolks and place in a blender. Chop whites and set aside. Cut bacon into ¼-inch julienne and fry in a skillet until crisp. Remove with a slotted spoon to paper towels. Add 1 tablespoon

of the bacon fat to the blender; discard the remainder. Cut onion in half crosswise and then slice lengthwise as thin as possible. Sprinkle onion over spinach.

3. Prepare vinaigrette by adding all remaining ingredients to the blender. Puree until smooth. Thin as necessary with water to keep it light in body. Dressing is best if made a day ahead. Bring to room temperature before using.

4. Serve salad by adding egg whites and bacon to bowl and spooning on about 2 tablespoons vinaigrette. Toss salad. Add more vinaigrette or vinegar to taste. If you prefer a wilted spinach salad, you may also heat the vinaigrette and add it to the spinach while still hot.

· · · · · · · ·

CHARRED GARLICKY SKIRT STEAKS

The Romans were among the first to appreciate skirt steaks. Until recently the steaks were usually ground up for hamburger, and no one wanted to eat this peculiar cut of beef. More recently they are appearing in the butcher's showcase, and they grill up to be tender and very flavorful steaks. If you have trouble finding skirt steaks, order them directly from your butcher. If you must substitute, a thin pounded flank steak should be your choice. When the coals are red-hot, cook the steaks quickly and aggressively, never cooking them beyond medium.

Serves 4

Approximately 4 pounds skirt steaks
6 cloves garlic, peeled
½ cup Kikkoman brand teriyaki sauce
¼ cup vegetable oil
½ teaspoon coarsely ground black pepper

1. Trim steaks by removing any of the thin "silverskin" found on the meat. Cut large pieces in half and pound well with a meat mallet. Using garlic press, squeeze garlic into a plastic food storage bag large enough to contain meat. Add teriyaki sauce, oil, and pepper. Add steaks, seal bag, and toss well. Marinate, refrigerated, overnight in bag.

2. Light a charcoal grill 30 minutes before dinnertime. When coals are at their hottest, char steaks on each side, turning once. Do not overcook, or steaks will dry out; they are best when medium-rare. Transfer to a warm serving platter to serve.

· · · · · · · ·

RED ONION RELISH

A quick preparation that adds depth to any grilled combination. Once you've prepared this, you can serve it while still steamy or spoon it into a jar and refrigerate it for the next grilling adventure.

Makes about 1 quart

4 medium-size red onions, peeled
⅓ cup olive oil
¼ cup thinly sliced garlic
3–4 bay leaves
1 tablespoon black peppercorns
2 tablespoons sugar

½ cup red wine vinegar
1 tablespoon dried thyme *or* 2 tablespoons fresh leaves
½ teaspoon hot red pepper flakes or to taste
½ teaspoon salt or to taste

1. Cut off ends of onions and cut each into eight wedges. In a heavy skillet, heat olive oil until smoky. Toss in onions, garlic, bay leaves, and black peppercorns and toss over high heat until onions are a vivid color, about 5 minutes. Sprinkle with sugar.

2. Add vinegar, thyme, and red pepper. Sauté quickly so most of the vinegar evaporates. Add salt to taste. The relish is done in just a few minutes, before onions become too soft. Serve immediately or pour into a glass jar along with juices. Cool to room temperature, then refrigerate. The relish is best when served warm.

· · · · · · · ·

GRILLED TOMATOES AND ROSEMARY POTATOES

I first had this wonderful combination years ago, and it's still a frequent course of my outdoor meals. The potatoes can be made slightly in advance, but the tomatoes are best when grilled right along with the entrée and served promptly. You'll find that the garlic and herb marinade comes in handy quite often and is perfect for all kinds of grilled meats, poultry, and vegetables.

Serves 4

⅓ cup extra-virgin olive oil
1 small onion, peeled and quartered
2 tablespoons fresh rosemary leaves
1 tablespoon fresh thyme leaves *or* 1 teaspoon dried
5 cloves garlic, peeled
1 teaspoon salt

½ teaspoon sugar
½ teaspoon freshly ground black pepper
8 small russet potatoes
4 medium-size ripe firm tomatoes
Additional extra-virgin olive oil, salt, sugar, and pepper

1. Preheat oven to 400°F. To make herb dressing, put ⅓ cup olive oil, onion, rosemary, thyme, garlic, salt, sugar, and pepper in a food processor. Puree until smooth. Scrape the marinade into a large bowl.

2. Scrub potatoes and cut them lengthwise into eighths. Place in a large roasting pan. Generously coat the potatoes with some of the herb dressing and toss them well. Arrange in a single layer in the pan and roast until brown and crisp, about 45 minutes, tossing potatoes around with a spatula every 10 minutes. When finished, remove to a serving platter, tent with foil, and keep warm until the steaks are done.

3. Begin grilling the tomatoes at the same time as the steaks. Cut them in half across the "belly" and sprinkle cut surfaces with a little additional olive oil, salt, sugar, and pepper. Lay them, cut side down, around the edges of the grill and cook until softened and "grill marks" are made. Don't try to pry the tomatoes free until they are completely cooked. Arrange cooked tomatoes in a serving dish and drizzle with some extra-virgin olive oil.

· · · · · · · ·

FRESH BLUEBERRY COBBLER WITH CINNAMON ICE CREAM

It's a remote spot indeed that doesn't get its share of summer's fresh blueberries. The Indians marked the beginning of summer with the appearance of the first bluish-purple berries. Here we enjoy them baked in a simple cobbler that's set off with cinnamon ice cream. You can substitute 3 cups of just about any other fresh fruit—for example, peaches, apples, strawberries, rhubarb, and combinations thereof—though nothing is quite like the blueberry.

Serves 6

4 cups (about 2 pints, picked over) fresh blueberries, washed
1 cup plus 3 tablespoons sugar
1 teaspoon fresh lemon juice
1 teaspoon ground cinnamon
¼ teaspoon ground cloves
1 cup all-purpose flour

1½ teaspoons baking powder
¼ teaspoon salt
½ cup (¼ pound) cold unsalted butter
¼ cup milk
1 egg
Cinnamon Ice Cream (recipe follows)

1. Combine blueberries, 1 cup sugar, lemon juice, cinnamon, and cloves in a large pot and simmer over medium heat until blueberries begin to become tender, about 3–5 minutes, stirring often. Remove from heat.

2. To prepare the topping, put flour, 3 tablespoons sugar, baking powder, and salt in a food processor and run machine for 2 seconds. Add cold butter and run machine for several seconds, until butter is cut through flour to resemble small peas.

3. Preheat oven to 400°F. Combine milk and egg in a small bowl and beat slightly with a fork. Pour egg mixture onto flour in processor and pulse machine just until ingredients are evenly moistened. Pour cooked filling into a 10-inch baking dish. Place cobbler topping over the surface with fingers, stretching dough over berries. Leave ample vent holes. Bake for 20–25 minutes, until brown and bubbly. Serve warm with Cinnamon Ice Cream.

CINNAMON ICE CREAM
Makes 1 quart

1½ cups milk
½ teaspoon ground cinnamon
1 cinnamon stick
⅔ cup sugar
3 egg yolks
Pinch of salt
1 cup whipping cream
1 tablespoon vanilla extract

1. Heat milk with ground cinnamon and cinnamon stick in a large saucepan until boiling; turn off heat. Add sugar and stir to dissolve. Allow to steep for 5 minutes.
2. In a bowl, beat egg yolks with a pinch of salt. Slowly stir about half the hot milk into the eggs. Return egg yolk mixture to milk in saucepan. Cook over medium heat, stirring constantly, until mixture thickens slightly and coats the back of a wooden spoon, about 5 minutes. Immediately remove from heat and pour through a strainer into a stainless-steel bowl. Add cream and vanilla. Chill thoroughly. Freeze in an ice cream maker according to manufacturer's instructions.

· · · · · · · ·

LA FIESTA

· · · · · · · ·

Guacamole and Corn Tortilla Chips

Chicken Enchilada Torta with Chili-Roasted Mole Sauce

Summer Vegetables with Lime Vinaigrette

Vanilla Caramel Flan and Fresh Berries

· · · · · · · ·

All dishes should be placed on the table together for this Mexican-style fiesta. Either margaritas or your favorite Mexican beer is the preferred beverage, though a large pitcher of lemonade is also a refreshing choice. The fiesta should be sampled at a leisurely pace so you can savor the flavors as they burst on your tongue.

GUACAMOLE AND CORN TORTILLA CHIPS

There are few pleasures more splendid than the flavor of a ripe avocado, as rich as butter with a whisper of anise. The secret to great guacamole is the ripeness of the avocado—the simplest way to test this is to stick a toothpick in the fruit at the stem end. If it flows freely in and out, the fruit is ready to use. If not, ripen it in a paper bag, at room temperature, for a day. It's best to make guacamole a few hours before eating, giving it enough time for flavors to develop. If you store guacamole overnight, its surface will likely discolor, which is harmless. Stir the guacamole and serve.

Serves 8

4 ripe avocados
¼ cup finely chopped cilantro leaves
2 small cloves garlic, smashed to a pulp
1 small white onion, peeled and minced fine
1–2 fresh jalapeño chilies, to taste, minced fine
¾ teaspoon salt or to taste

Juice of 2 limes
2 dashes of Tabasco sauce or to taste
1 large ripe tomato, diced fine, juice discarded
Cilantro sprig for garnish
Vegetable oil for frying chips
12 corn tortillas or blue corn tortillas, cut into wedges

1. Peel avocados, remove and discard pits, and place avocado in a large stainless-steel bowl. Add cilantro, garlic, onion, chilies, salt, lime juice, and Tabasco and mash

together with a large whisk, taking care not to puree the avocados. A good guacamole should be light, chunky, and flavorful. Fold in the chopped tomato. Garnish with a sprig of cilantro.

2. To make chips, heat 1 inch oil to 375°F in a medium-size saucepan. Fry tortillas until lightly golden, about 30 seconds. Drain on paper towels and serve with guacamole.

· · · · · · · ·

CHICKEN ENCHILADA TORTA
WITH CHILI-ROASTED MOLE SAUCE

This is sort of a Mexican lasagna that's layered with spicy homemade mole sauce and other assorted condiments. If you're a chili eater and like food to burst on your tongue, feel free to add a jalapeño or serrano chili or two. The sauce is best when you make at least two quarts. You'll need one for the torta; the other can be frozen and used for simple enchiladas someday.

Serves 8 (2 quarts sauce)

MOLE SAUCE
½ pound ancho chilies
1 ounce guajillo chilies
1 ounce cascabel chilies
1 cup chopped onion
6 cloves garlic, peeled and minced
2 tablespoons olive oil
1 pound (6–8) Roma-style (plum) tomatoes
2 teaspoons ground cumin
2 teaspoons dried leaf oregano
1½ tablespoons salt or to taste
½ teaspoon ground cinnamon
½ teaspoon ground allspice
2 tablespoons sugar
2 ounces semisweet chocolate

CHICKEN ENCHILADA TORTA
½ pound poblano chilies
4 pounds chicken thighs, skin removed
12 corn tortillas
1 pound frozen corn kernels, rinsed with hot water and drained
1 pound Monterey Jack cheese, shredded (about 4 cups)
4 medium-size scallions, sliced thin
3 tablespoons chopped cilantro
2 cups sour cream
Cilantro sprigs for garnish

1. To make the sauce, preheat the broiler and toast all the dried chilies under the broiler in a cast-iron skillet until soft and pliable. Toast the poblanos in a similar fashion until skins are charred black. While still warm, remove seeds and veins from dried chilies and black skin and stems from poblanos, wearing rubber gloves; do not rinse under running water. Set poblanos aside. Simmer dried chilies in a pot of water for 20 minutes, until soft. Remove chilies, reserving water.

2. Meanwhile, sauté onion and garlic in oil over medium-low heat until tender, about 10 minutes. Roast tomatoes about 6 inches under broiler for about 10 minutes, turning several times.

3. Place chilies in blender. Add tomatoes, onions, garlic, seasonings, and sugar. Add 1 cup of the chili water. Puree to a fine paste by adding liquid as necessary; you may have to do this in two batches. Pour the sauce into a large pot, add chocolate, and simmer to melt. Thin sauce with water until it's the consistency of barbecue sauce. Sauce may be made the day before and refrigerated.

4. To prepare the torta, place 1 quart of the sauce in a large saucepan. Add chicken, cover, and simmer until tender, about 30 minutes. Remove chicken and allow to cool.

5. Preheat oven to 425°F. Remove chicken from bones and cut into small strips. Cut eight of the tortillas in half through the diameter. Place four tortilla halves around the outer edges of a 10-inch springform pan. Place a whole tortilla in center. Spread ½ cup sauce over tortillas. Lay one-third of the chicken, corn, cheese, scallions, and cilantro on the sauce. Spread another ½ cup sauce over top. Repeat layering until all ingredients are used, ending with a top layer of tortillas. Arrange poblano chilies over top. Cover with aluminum foil and place on a baking sheet. Bake for 35 minutes. Remove from oven and cool on a rack for 10 minutes. Remove sides of pan and cut torta into wedges. Serve with a dollop of sour cream and spring of cilantro. Extra sauce freezes well.

· · · · · · · ·

SUMMER VEGETABLES WITH LIME VINAIGRETTE

Summer is when the markets are filled with the greatest selection of vegetables. Any combination you choose is enhanced by this tart lime dressing. Take care not to overcook the vegetables. They should be quite cold and crisp when served.

Serves 8

½ cup extra-virgin olive oil
½ bunch scallions, white parts only
3 cloves garlic, peeled
2 tablespoons cilantro leaves
2 tablespoons fresh lime juice
1 tablespoon rice wine vinegar
Grated zest of 1 lime
3 teaspoons sugar
½ teaspoon salt or to taste
½ teaspoon freshly ground black pepper
   or to taste

5 carrots, peeled and cut on the bias into
   1-inch pieces
½ pound fresh green beans, ends snapped
   off
1 bunch broccoli, trimmed to flowerets
1 head cauliflower, trimmed to flowerets
1 red bell pepper, seeds removed, sliced
   into ¼-inch strips
3 yellow summer squash, cut into
   lengthwise quarters

1. Prepare dressing in advance by combining all ingredients except vegetables in a blender and pureeing until smooth. Refrigerate. Shake well before using.

2. Steam vegetables in the order in which they will cook, beginning with carrots. Add green beans, broccoli, and cauliflower after a few minutes, then pepper and squash. Cook only until just done; keep them firm. Plunge the vegetables into ice water and remove to a colander. Toss with paper towels to remove moisture and refrigerate until thoroughly chilled.

3. To serve, place vegetables in a large bowl and pour on a little of the dressing. Toss, adding more dressing to taste. Serve vegetables by themselves or with tossed lettuces.

· · · · · · · ·

VANILLA CARAMEL FLAN AND FRESH BERRIES

This simple caramel flan accompanied by summer blueberries and raspberries is the perfect way to extinguish the flames from a Mexican food fiesta. The cool custard must be made the day before, giving the caramel time to dissolve into the sweet syrup that glazes the flan.

Serves 8

1 cup sugar
2 tablespoons water
2 tablespoons maple syrup
1 vanilla bean
2½ cups milk
3 eggs
3 egg yolks
Pinch of freshly grated nutmeg
1 teaspoon vanilla extract
Approximately 1½ pints assorted summer
　berries

1. Prepare the caramel by combining ½ cup of the sugar, water, and maple syrup in a small saucepan over medium-high heat. Stir with a wooden spoon for about 3 minutes, until syrup begins to turn light brown and caramelize. Immediately pour it over the bottom of a 1-quart glass ovenproof dish and tilt in all directions to coat the bottom evenly. Set aside.

2. To make the custard, split the vanilla bean lengthwise and combine with milk in a saucepan over medium heat. Bring to a boil and remove from heat. Scrape seeds out of bean and return both seeds and bean to milk.

3. Preheat oven to 325°F. In a small mixing bowl, combine remaining ½ cup sugar with eggs and egg yolks and beat until foamy. Add nutmeg. Remove vanilla bean from hot milk and slowly drizzle milk into eggs. Add vanilla extract. Pour custard through a strainer into the baking dish. Place dish in a large pan on the bottom rack of the oven and pour into the pan enough hot water to come halfway up sides of dish. Bake for 45 minutes, then check to see if a knife comes out clean when inserted in the center. If not, continue baking for 5 minutes and check again.

4. When done, remove flan from water bath and allow to cool to room temperature. Refrigerate overnight. To unmold, loosen the sides with a knife, cover the top with a serving platter, and quickly invert the custard. Allow the caramel sauce to run over top. Arrange an assortment of summer berries around the sides.

· · · · · · · ·

BACKYARD BARBECUE

· · · · · · · ·

Roasted Eggplant and Red Onion Salad

Chilled Lemon Pasta with Summer Zucchini, Tomato, and Fresh Basil

*Barbecued Free-Range Chicken and Baby Back Ribs
with Secret Killer Barbecue Sauce*

Pasadena Nectarine Pie

· · · · · · · ·

ROASTED EGGPLANT AND RED ONION SALAD

Eggplant is a most neglected vegetable. Despite the homely designation, it is one of my favorite vegetables and is the basis of this wonderful salad. It's important to use the very best olive oil when making this salad. You'll also find it's best if prepared the day before, allowing the onions and garlic to soften and mellow. It works perfectly at a barbecue since it can be made ahead of time, served at room temperature, and requires no extra fuss. Serve with toasted pita bread wedges, breadsticks, or sesame crackers.

Serves 4–6

1 large eggplant
Juice of 2 lemons
3 vine-ripened tomatoes, cut into small
  dice
1 bunch Italian (flat-leaf) parsley,
  chopped (about ¾ cup)
3 cloves garlic, peeled and put through a
  press

½ teaspoon salt or to taste
¼ cup extra-virgin olive oil
½ teaspoon freshly ground black pepper
  or to taste
1 medium-size red onion, peeled and
  diced fine

1. Preheat oven to 450°F. Place unpeeled whole eggplant in a small metal baking pan and roast for 1 hour or until eggplant is charred and completely soft, turning it every 15 minutes to blacken all sides evenly. Allow the eggplant to cool for 10 minutes, then peel it while still hot. Tear the eggplant into small to medium-size pieces with your fingers and place them in a colander. Place colander on a plate and refrigerate for several hours or overnight, allowing bitter liquids to drain.

2. To complete salad, combine eggplant with remaining ingredients. Toss and season well with salt and pepper. Refrigerate to allow flavors to mellow. Serve chilled or at room temperature.

· · · · · · · ·

CHILLED LEMON PASTA WITH SUMMER ZUCCHINI, TOMATO, AND FRESH BASIL

The dried pasta you purchase for this chilled summer salad should be a small-cut version, such as penne, ziti, or farfalle.

Serves 4–6

6 quarts water
1 pound dried short-cut pasta
Juice of 2 lemons
⅓ cup extra-virgin olive oil
3 small green zucchini
3 small yellow zucchini or crookneck squash
4 cloves garlic, peeled and minced
2 pounds ripe Roma-style (plum) tomatoes, peeled and seeded (see Index)

¼ cup (about ½ bunch) finely shredded fresh basil leaves
½ teaspoon salt or to taste
½ teaspoon sugar or to taste
½ teaspoon freshly ground black pepper or to taste

1. Bring 6 quarts salted water to a boil. Boil pasta until al dente, drain in a colander, and rinse quickly with cold water. Place in a large bowl and immediately squeeze lemon juice through a strainer onto pasta, tossing well. Add half the olive oil and toss again. Set aside.

2. Slice all zucchini in half lengthwise, then into ¼-inch slices on the bias. Heat remaining olive oil in a large skillet over medium-high heat. Add zucchini and sauté quickly until tender, just a minute or 2. Add garlic and cook for another minute. Add tomatoes and swirl the skillet around. Add basil, salt, sugar, and pepper, seasoning generously since the vegetables will be combined with the pasta. After a minute or 2, pour vegetables over pasta and toss everything together. Taste and correct seasoning. Serve chilled or at room temperature.

· · · · · · · ·

BARBECUED FREE-RANGE CHICKEN
AND BABY BACK RIBS
WITH SECRET KILLER BARBECUE SAUCE

Free-range refers to the fact that these chickens are allowed to roam the barnyard (range) freely rather than being pent up in a coop and filled with chemicals and hormones. The taste and quality distinction is immediate, so I always endorse free-range over any other kind. I'm really not sure which is the "secret" ingredient in this barbecue sauce, since they all contribute to its pungent flavor. It's important to precook both the chicken and the ribs, since this barbecue sauce contains a lot of sugar that blackens too quickly to do all the cooking on the grill. If it's simply too hot to light the oven, slowly grill the meats on the barbecue instead, without precooking and without barbecue sauce, simply sprinkled with salt and pepper. When almost done, begin to paint liberally and frequently with barbecue sauce and continue until browned and crisp. Both the chicken and the ribs may be precooked the day before and refrigerated *without* sauce. The next day, toss with sauce and grill.

Serves 6 (About 1 quart size)

¼ cup vegetable oil
1 medium-size onion, minced fine
⅓ cup minced garlic
1 14-ounce bottle ketchup
1 12-ounce bottle chili sauce
1 tablespoon liquid smoke flavoring
1 heaped cup dark brown sugar
2 tablespoons Worcestershire sauce
2 tablespoons hot red pepper flakes or to
     taste
1 cup strong brewed coffee
¾ cup red wine vinegar or cider vinegar
2 teaspoons salt
1 teaspoon freshly ground black pepper
2 slabs baby back ribs
2 2-pound fryer chickens, cut up

1. To prepare barbecue sauce, heat the oil in a large saucepan and add onion and garlic. Cook over medium-high heat for a minute or two, then add remaining ingredients except ribs and chicken. Simmer for 15 minutes. Taste sauce; it should be quite strong and spicy to properly marinate the meats. Remove from heat and cool.

2. Cut each slab of ribs into three equal sections. Place them in a large pot, cover with cold water, add a little salt, and cook at a low simmer for about 50 minutes, until bones are *almost* coming free from meat. Meanwhile, preheat oven to 425°F and arrange chicken on a rack in a roasting pan. Roast for 45 minutes, until it's almost completely cooked. Transfer both the ribs and chicken to a large bowl and, while still hot, toss or paint them heavily with the barbecue sauce. Allow to marinate until barbecuing time.

3. Light a charcoal grill about 30 minutes before barbecuing time; the coals should be past their hottest point. Place the ribs and chicken on the grill and cook slowly, basting frequently with additional barbecue sauce. When charred and crispy, remove to serving platter and serve.

· · · · · · · ·

PASADENA NECTARINE PIE

Nectarines are neither a cross between a peach and a plum nor a fuzzless peach. They are their own distinct variety of fruit, virtually all of which are grown in California. A select few are nurtured in a friend's yard in the sunny city of Pasadena, and each season, with some special care and a bit of spice, she bakes them into this scrumptious, bubbling pie.

Serves 6 (1 9-inch pie)

3⅓ cups all-purpose flour
1 teaspoon salt
1 cup plus 2 teaspoons sugar
1 cup (½ pound) unsalted butter, cut into
    small pieces and frozen
½ cup or more ice water
Approximately 5 cups pitted and sliced
    nectarines
½ teaspoon ground cinnamon
½ teaspoon ground ginger
2 tablespoons unsalted butter, sliced thin
1 egg white, lightly beaten
1 egg
2 tablespoons heavy cream
Additional sugar for sprinkling in pie

1. Prepare crust by mixing together 3 cups of the flour, the salt, and 2 teaspoons of the sugar in a food processor. Add frozen butter and pulse machine until butter is cut to the size of small peas. Drizzle ½ cup ice water over the mixture and pulse

51

again to bring the mass together. If it seems too dry, add a bit more water. Turn out on floured surface, divide in two, and form two flat disks, each about 5 inches in diameter. Chill for 15 minutes.

2. Preheat oven to 400°F. Lay one piece of dough on a floured sheet of wax paper. Flour it lightly on top and cover with another sheet of wax paper. Roll it out to an 11-inch circle, about $\frac{1}{8}$ inch thick. Discard the top layer of wax paper and invert dough into a 9-inch pie plate. Press dough lightly into the plate, remove paper, and trim the sides $\frac{1}{4}$ inch beyond rim. Bake for 5 minutes. Remove from oven and allow to cool. Meanwhile, roll out remaining dough to a 13-inch circle, in a similar fashion. Remove paper, then cut the circle into 12 wedges, lay them on a cookie sheet, and refrigerate.

3. Preheat oven to 425°F. In a large bowl, combine nectarines, remaining 1 cup sugar, remaining $\frac{1}{3}$ cup flour, cinnamon, and ginger. Toss well to coat nectarines. Fill precooked pie shell and dot with sliced butter. Moisten rim of the piecrust with egg white and lay on each of the chilled pastry wedges, points toward the center and slightly overlapping each other, in a circle over pie. Paint egg white on all pastry seams and lightly press them together; press the edges of the top and bottom crust together as well. Trim around rim. Fold back center points of top crust, exposing a 2-inch circle of nectarines in the center.

4. Beat the egg with the cream and paint the pie. Sprinkle with additional sugar and bake for 15 minutes. Reduce heat to 350°F and bake for 30–35 minutes. Cool on a wire rack. Serve warm or at room temperature.

· · · · · · · ·

THE PICNIC

········

Crusty Herb Bread and Kalamata Olive Tapenade

Roasted Red Peppers with Slivered Garlic and Basil

San Domenico Chicken Liver Pâté

Grandma's Dill Pickles

Walnut Fried Chicken Drumettes with Roquefort Yogurt Dressing

Italian Almond Biscotti

Cocoa Pepper Cookies

········

Whether you unpack your ingredients and utensils in a sunny field or at a concert under the stars, a picnic should be very special. Summer outings are, however, best when kept informal, so plan your picnic thoroughly for an easy and relaxing experience. Choose foods that are at their best at room temperature so they can be enjoyed casually throughout the picnic—events such as this one are nibblers, intended for continuous grazing and munching. Since everything on a picnic is laid out at the same time, it's important that the foods be colorful and appetizing. Depending on the number of picnic participants, you may take along only a small quantity of each menu item, refrigerating the rest for another day. And don't forget, no summer picnic is complete without an assortment of ripe fresh fruit.

CRUSTY HERB BREAD AND KALAMATA OLIVE TAPENADE

We began baking this bread at the restaurant years ago in a small pizza oven, and I have since had countless requests for this recipe—making bread at home seems to have become a welcome chore. Now, at the bakery, we bake thousands of loaves a day in a large stone-lined oven. The loaves are still placed directly on the oven hearth, which causes them to rise quickly and blossom open. It's important to lay the loaves directly on a hot surface—at home you will get the best results from baking them on a special pizza stone, on unglazed quarry tiles, or, if you must, on a preheated metal baking sheet. If you do use the baking sheet, the loaves may not open quite as prettily as they do at the bakery, but the flavor and texture will certainly be as wonderful. This recipe requires fresh herbs since they are more aromatic than their dried counterparts and lend an attractive green speckle to the baked loaves.

Makes 3 large loaves

1 cup hot tap water
1 cup water
2 ¼-ounce packages active dry yeast
1 small onion, peeled
6 cloves garlic, peeled
Leaves from 1 12-inch sprig fresh
   rosemary (about ¼ cup)
¼ cup fresh thyme leaves
2½ tablespoons extra-virgin olive oil
1 tablespoon salt
7 cups bread flour
Additional olive oil for oiling dough

1. Pour the hot water into a large electric mixer bowl. Sprinkle on dry yeast; wait 1 minute, then mix to dissolve. Fit mixer with dough hook attachment.

2. Meanwhile, put onion and garlic in blender with remaining cup of water. Add herbs and blend until very smooth, about 30 seconds. Add to yeast mixture. Add 2½ tablespoons oil and the salt.

3. Add 6 cups of the flour and start mixing at low speed. When flour is incorporated, turn mixture to medium speed and knead for 7 minutes. Add the remaining flour as necessary to prevent dough from sticking to bowl. It should be quite firm. Occasionally redistribute dough in bowl if necessary. At the end of the kneading time, oil sides of a large bowl with some olive oil, oil dough lightly, place in bowl, and cover top of dough loosely with plastic wrap. Allow to rise in a warm, draft-free place for 45 minutes.

4. After rising time, turn dough out onto a floured board and knead for 1 minute. Cut into three equal pieces and dust each with flour. Form each round by turning dough inside itself with fingertips, stretching down the sides and tucking it underneath the loaf, dipping fingers in flour to prevent sticking. Rounds should be tightly formed. Roll loaves very heavily in flour, especially on the bottom, place them on a baking sheet, and allow them to rise for 45 minutes, covered with a kitchen towel, in a warm, draft-free place. (You may also proof and bake the loaves in baking pans.)

5. Place a pizza stone in the oven and allow ample time to preheat oven to 450°F. Slice a cross into the tops of the loaves with a razor blade, cutting about ½ inch

deep. Place them directly on the preheated cooking surface in the oven. Bake for 30 minutes or until loaves are very brown and hollow-sounding when tapped. Loaves keep fresh at room temperature for 1 day. Otherwise, place loaf in freezer without wrapping. When frozen, place in a tightly sealed plastic bag. Reheat in a 400°F oven.

To mix dough by hand:
1. Pour 1 cup hot tap water into a very large bowl. Sprinkle on dry yeast; wait 1 minute, then mix to dissolve.

2. Prepare onion/herb mixture as in main directions. Add to yeast mixture. Add 2½ tablespoons oil and the salt. Gradually add 6 cups of flour, 1 cup at a time, mixing with a spoon until dough becomes firm enough to knead. Invert onto kneading surface and knead by hand until smooth and elastic, about 12 minutes. Add more flour as necessary to form a firm dough.

3. Lightly oil dough and place in an oiled bowl. Cover loosely with plastic wrap and allow to rise in a warm, draft-free place for 1 hour. Proceed with step 4.

KALAMATA OLIVE TAPENADE
Serves 6

1 2-ounce can anchovy fillets, rinsed well
   under running water
½ cup black Kalamata or other Greek-
   style black olives, pits removed
¼ cup drained capers
¼ cup extra-virgin olive oil
1 clove garlic, peeled
1 tablespoon Dijon mustard
¼ teaspoon freshly ground black pepper

In a food processor, blend all ingredients until a smooth paste forms. If the tapenade seems too thick to dip bread into, add more olive oil and blend for a few more seconds. Serve at room temperature. Keeps refrigerated for weeks.

· · · · · · · ·

ROASTED RED PEPPERS WITH SLIVERED GARLIC AND BASIL

When the summer heat is at its greatest and green bell peppers are abundant, farmers allow a portion of their crop to become fully ripe and turn vivid red, and we begin to see them appear at the market. In California they've become such a favorite that farmers are allowing more and more of the greens to ripen. America also gets a good-size shipment from Mexico and other countries that send us not only red but also yellow, purple, orange, and even brown bell peppers at different times of the year.

Serves 6

¼ cup extra-virgin olive oil
5 cloves garlic, peeled and sliced as thin
  as possible
5 medium-size red bell peppers
Approximately 6 fresh basil leaves
Red wine vinegar or balsamic vinegar to
  taste (optional)

1. Heat olive oil in a small saucepan and add garlic. Cook slowly over very low heat until garlic is soft and sweet, about 8 minutes. Set aside.

2. Roast peppers over an open flame on top of the stove or under a preheated electric broiler, until the skin is charred and black. As they are done, place in a plastic bag and seal. Allow to steam for 5 minutes. While peppers are hot, cut in half and remove stem and seeds. Peel the charred skin off the peppers at the sink, rinsing your fingertips, not the pepper, under cold running water. For best flavor, do not rinse them after you've peeled away the skin. Tear them into long strips and arrange on a platter or in a bowl. Sprinkle with a pinch of salt and lay the basil leaves over the surface.

3. Pour the warm oil and garlic onto the peppers and basil and allow them to marinate at room temperature for an hour. Or refrigerate for up to 1 week, then serve at room temperature. You may also like a drizzle of red wine vinegar or balsamic vinegar on them before serving.

· · · · · · · ·

SAN DOMENICO CHICKEN LIVER PATE

Here's a recipe I learned while working at the San Domenico restaurant in Italy. Like almost everything else made there, it's a triumph of fine cuisine. This pâté is subtle in flavor and is a delicate dish, so follow these directions carefully—a small deviation could ruin it. If you prefer, you may spoon the pâté into a pastry bag and decorate tiny toasts or even pipe it into small individual crocks and decorate them with green peppercorns, sliced truffle, or a leaf of parsley. For a simple pasta sauce, add a few spoons of the pâté to a basic cream sauce and season with salt and pepper. Boil dry pasta, drain, and toss with the sauce, thinning it out with a little milk if necessary. Heaven!

Makes about 3 cups, serving 6–8

1½ cups (¾ pound) unsalted butter,
    slightly softened and cut into small
    slices
4 large bay leaves
1¼ pounds chicken livers, washed well
    and picked free of membrane
1 teaspoon salt plus additional to taste
½ teaspoon freshly ground white pepper
¼ cup brandy plus additional to taste
¼ cup marsala

1. Heat a large skillet over high heat. Add about 3 tablespoons of the butter and the bay leaves. Allow leaves to sizzle in the butter until hot, then add chicken livers. Sauté lightly for 1 minute over high heat, then lower heat and allow livers to simmer for 5 minutes. Sprinkle them with salt and white pepper.

2. Turn heat to high and add 2 tablespoons of the brandy and 2 tablespoons of the marsala; you may flame the brandy if you have an appreciative audience, though it's really not necessary. Swirl pan around over heat for about 2 minutes, until juices have evaporated to leave only the butter. Remove bay leaves and set aside. Cool for a few minutes, then refrigerate until butter is firm and livers are chilled.

3. Scrape chilled livers along with the butter and juice into a food processor. Add remaining softened butter and run machine to puree the mixture, scraping down sides of bowl. While machine is running, add remaining brandy and marsala. Season with additional salt and brandy to taste.

4. Pack the pâté into a crock and arrange the reserved bay leaves on top. Press plastic wrap over surface and refrigerate. Soften pâté almost to room temperature before serving and serve as you would butter with bread. This pâté freezes well.

. . . .

GRANDMA'S DILL PICKLES

This is still my favorite pickle, maybe because of its crunchy crispness and lusty flavor or maybe because of memories of Grandma's cellar and the wooden shelves lined with pickle jars. She would pick a bushel of the small, special cucumbers at the end of the summer and immediately begin the canning process, making pickles for family and friends and for use throughout the year. Don't even think of making these pickles if you can't find fresh dill flowers and seed heads. If you request it from the produce buyer at your local grocery, it can usually be found sometime during the summer. When the canning jars are sealed properly, the lid caves inward. If a lid doesn't seal properly after it's cooled, it will puff up, meaning the vacuum was not made. If this happens, put the dud in the refrigerator for a couple of weeks to marinate, then enjoy the pickles.

Makes 4 quarts

5–6 pounds small pickling cucumbers
Approximately ⅓ cup plus 4 teaspoons salt
1 bunch fresh dill, flowers only
6 tablespoons sugar

4 pinches of hot red pepper flakes
1 teaspoon ground turmeric
8 cloves garlic, peeled and sliced thin
2⅔ cups white vinegar
2 teaspoons dill seed

1. Scrub cucumbers with a bristol brush. Plug sink and add enough cold water to cover. Sprinkle heavily with salt and soak for 1 hour.

2. Wash 4 1-quart canning jars in soap and hot water or in the dishwasher. While they are still hot, place a dill flower in the bottom of each jar. Divide the remaining ingredients among jars as well. Pack cucumbers in jars vertically, continuing to fill to the top, inserting dill flowers here and there. Cut in half if necessary to fill spaces. Add tap water to cover. Place cap on each jar and tighten securely.

3. In a large pot, place jars on a rack and fill to top of jars with hot water. Over medium-high heat, bring water to a gentle boil; then cook for 2 minutes. Remove jars from water bath and invert them onto a cloth. Very gently rock the jars to dissolve any undissolved seasoning. Store upside down overnight. The next day, turn upright and remove rings. The seals should be sucked downward, ensuring that a proper vacuum has taken place. Allow to sit for at least 1 month in a cool place free from direct sunlight. Very gently shake jars once a week to redistribute brine. Sealed pickles stay crisp for up to a year stored at room temperature. Refrigerate after opening.

· · · · · · · ·

WALNUT FRIED CHICKEN DRUMETTES
WITH ROQUEFORT YOGURT DRESSING

The drumette is the large joint of the wing that resembles a miniature drumstick. It can often be purchased in supermarket packages. If you can't find drumettes, buy whole wings, disjoint them, and reserve the tip and middle part for making chicken soup. Lots of folk around Buffalo, New York, have been chomping down piles of these "wing-dings," as they call them, dipped in basic Roquefort dressing. Once I tried walnuts in the breading, chilled the wings, and made a lighter, yogurt-based dressing for a change and discovered an absolutely terrific reason to go on a picnic.

Makes 24 (2½ cups dressing)

24 chicken drumettes
2 cups buttermilk
1 cup all-purpose flour
2 cups chopped walnuts
1½ teaspoons salt
¼ teaspoon cayenne pepper
½ teaspoon freshly ground black pepper

½ teaspoon paprika
Vegetable oil for frying
1 bunch celery, trimmed and sliced into sticks
Roquefort Yogurt Dressing (recipe follows)

1. Wash the drumettes and place them in a large bowl; cover with buttermilk. Let chicken soak for at least 1 hour, refrigerated.

2. Meanwhile, combine flour, walnuts, salt, cayenne, pepper, and paprika in a food processor. Process until fine. Coat each drumette thoroughly with flour and walnut mixture. Place them on a rack and air-dry for 15 minutes before frying.

3. Preheat oven to 350°F. Heat an inch of vegetable oil in a large skillet and fry each drumette until crisp and browned on all sides, about 3–5 minutes. Place them on a rack on a baking sheet and put them in the oven until meat easily comes free from bone, about 15 minutes. Eat while hot, at room temperature, or chilled. Serve with celery sticks and dressing.

ROQUEFORT YOGURT DRESSING

1 cup mayonnaise
½ cup plain yogurt
⅓ cup crumbled Roquefort cheese
2–3 tablespoons buttermilk
2 cloves garlic, peeled

1 tablespoon white wine vinegar
1 teaspoon salt
½ teaspoon freshly ground black pepper
¼ teaspoon cayenne pepper
¼ cup chopped chives

Place all ingredients except chives in a blender, using 2 tablespoons buttermilk. Process until smooth. Stir in chives. Chill until ready to serve. Thin with more buttermilk if desired when ready to serve.

. . . .

59

ITALIAN ALMOND BISCOTTI

These cookies were as much a staple as flour and sugar in my family. They were always around, whether coffee was being served or wine was being drunk. After you've tried these biscotti, you'll probably want to double the recipe the next time. They go quickly.

Makes about 5 dozen

3 eggs
¾ cup sugar
2–2¼ cups all-purpose flour
2 teaspoons baking powder
¼ teaspoon salt
1 tablespoon bourbon
2 tablespoons vegetable oil
½ teaspoon aniseed
2 teaspoons grated lemon zest
2 teaspoons lemon extract
2 cups shelled almonds

1. Preheat oven to 350°F. In the bowl of an electric mixer, beat eggs and sugar together until thick and velvety. Meanwhile, sift together 2 cups of the flour, the baking powder, and the salt. Turn mixer to low speed and add bourbon, oil, aniseed, lemon zest, and extract. Add flour a little at a time, incorporating it and adding as much as you need to make a sticky dough. Remove bowl from mixer and stir in almonds.

2. Turn dough out onto a floured work surface and divide into three equal pieces. Roll each piece into a 1½-inch-thick log, oiling your hands to prevent sticking. Place logs on a nonstick 8″ × 12″ baking sheet. Bake for 20 minutes. Transfer the logs to a cutting surface using two spatulas. Allow to cool completely.

3. Increase oven temperature to 400°F. Slice logs ½ inch thick on the bias, using a very sharp serrated knife. Take your time and saw through the nuts. Lay the cookies flat on the baking sheet and bake them for 8–10 minutes, until the edges brown. Remove them from sheet immediately and cool on racks. Cookies may be kept in an airtight container for 1 week at room temperature or frozen for up to 1 month.

· · · · · · · ·

COCOA PEPPER COOKIES

These were always my favorite cookies that Grandma Til used to make. The fact that they contained pepper, of all things, made them seem intriguing and exotic to me, and I used to sit and eat these spiced, cocoa-flavored cookies until my glass of milk ran dry. While writing this book, I prepared the cookies for the first time, since Grandma always used to do it, and I found myself sitting, once again, with a glass of milk. The cookies are more cakelike than fudgy, and you'll find they are great when served with coffee as well.

Makes 5 dozen

COOKIES
3 cups all-purpose flour, sifted
1 cup sugar
1 teaspoon ground cinnamon
1 teaspoon freshly ground black pepper
½ teaspoon ground cloves
¼ teaspoon salt
½ cup unsweetened cocoa powder
3 teaspoons baking powder
½ cup (¼ pound) unsalted butter, chilled
   and sliced
3 extra-large eggs
½ cup milk
1 teaspoon vanilla extract

GLAZE
1 cup confectioners' sugar
¼ teaspoon ground cinnamon
¼ teaspoon vanilla extract
Approximately 1 tablespoon milk

1. Place all dry ingredients for cookies in a large bowl and mix very well with a wire whisk. Cut the butter slices into the dry ingredients with a pastry blender or two knives, as you would for a pie crust, until it has a very coarse grain.

2. Beat together the eggs, milk, and vanilla. Add to flour and butter mixture and stir to make a soft dough. Turn out on a work surface and form a ball; knead just until dry ingredients are moistened. Handle lightly. The dough should be veined with butter.

3. Preheat oven to 350°F. Roll out sections of the dough into long snakelike pieces, ¾ inch in diameter. Cut them into 1-inch slices with a sharp knife and place them on a baking sheet. Bake for 8–10 minutes, until set; do not overbake. Remove to a rack to cool. Refrigerate unrolled dough while baking cookies.

4. To glaze cookies, stir together all glaze ingredients, using enough milk to make a drizzling consistency. Dip tops of cookies into icing. Store in refrigerator in a sealed plastic container.

A U T U M N

Crisp air and changing leaves signal the flavors of autumn. With harvest time approaching, summer peppers turn bright red, squashes swell, and muscat grapes become as sweet as honey. As the air becomes colder, ovens are lit for roasting and baking, steaming the windows and filling the house with enticing aromas.

HARVEST MOON

. . . .

*Steamed Broccoli Salad with Extra-Virgin Olive Oil
and Dijon Vinaigrette*

Stuffed Breast of Chicken with Sage and Corn Bread

Hot Apple Cider

Raspberry Linzer Cookies

. . . .

STEAMED BROCCOLI SALAD WITH EXTRA-VIRGIN OLIVE OIL AND DIJON VINAIGRETTE

Here's a simple way to prepare broccoli, a staple companion to any meal. I've always liked broccoli cooked softer than most people; it's what I got used to as a child. You should, of course, steam the broccoli as long as you like, but remember that it will continue to cook when removed from the heat.

Serves 6

3 tablespoons extra-virgin olive oil
1 teaspoon Dijon mustard
½ teaspoon salt or to taste
¼ teaspoon freshly ground black pepper
   or to taste
½ teaspoon sugar
2 bunches broccoli
Juice of ½ lemon (optional)

1. Combine oil, mustard, and seasonings in a large bowl. Blend with fork.

2. Cut off flowerets of broccoli, trim stems, and wash well. Steam or boil for a few minutes until broccoli is cooked to desired tenderness. Drain well. While hot, place in bowl with dressing and toss well. Serve immediately or at room temperature as a salad. Retoss with fresh lemon juice before serving if desired.

. . . .

STUFFED BREAST OF CHICKEN WITH SAGE AND CORN BREAD

This is the entrée to prepare for a crowd, since it can be preroasted, then finished for serving after you've cleaned up the kitchen and lit the candles. Purchase or make a quick corn bread the day before, allowing it to dry out a bit, helping the stuffing hold together. A side dish of Cranberry Pear Relish (see Index) adds color and spirit to the plate, its tartness complementing the sweet corn bread stuffing.

Serves 6

3 cups coarsely crumbled corn bread (1 loaf)
¼ cup unsalted butter
1 medium-size onion, chopped fine
1 stalk celery, chopped fine, with some leaves
¼ cup minced fresh sage, *or* 2 tablespoons dried
½ cup chopped Italian (flat-leaf) parsley
¼ cup chopped toasted pecans (optional)

½ cup or more chicken broth
½ teaspoon salt or to taste
½ teaspoon freshly ground black pepper or to taste
6 large boneless chicken breast halves, with skin
Extra-virgin olive oil for basting
1 cup dry white wine

1. Prepare stuffing by crumbling corn bread into a large bowl. Heat the butter in a medium-size skillet and sweat the onion and celery over medium-high heat until soft and transparent but not colored—about 8 minutes. Add the sage, parsley, and pecans. Cook for 1 minute and add ½ cup chicken broth, salt, and pepper. Remove from heat and pour over corn bread. Toss well, wetting all bread, adding more broth as necessary to make a moist stuffing.

2. Preheat oven to 450°F. Pound each chicken breast half between two sheets of plastic wrap, skin down, until flattened. Remove from plastic, place skin down on a cutting board, and sprinkle with salt and pepper. Mound about ½ cup of the stuffing over the breast, lift up the sides over the stuffing, and secure them with a metal skewer, weaving it through the skin. Place the breast, skewer down, in a roasting pan. Repeat with other breasts.

3. Paint them liberally with olive oil, sprinkle lightly with salt and pepper, and roast, uncovered, for about 15 minutes. Baste with olive oil, then cook for 10 minutes more. Remove pan from oven, add wine, and cover with aluminum foil. At this point you may continue to roast for about 20 minutes more, until breasts are cooked, depending on size, and serve immediately, or keep them at room temperature for up to 2 hours and finish roasting at 450°F for another 15 minutes or until a meat thermometer reads 185°F. Serve with wine drippings spooned over top.

. . . .

65

HOT APPLE CIDER

In midautumn, when the harvest is at its peak, apples abound. This is the time when the cider is made, the best of which always seems to appear on the side of a quiet country road. Depending on how sweet it is, you may want to add a spoon of brown sugar to the mulling. I also like to add a shot or two of rum to each mug right before serving.

Serves 6

1 orange
1 cinnamon stick
3 cloves
6 cups apple cider
2 tablespoons light brown sugar
   (optional)
1½ cups dark rum (optional)

Remove peel from orange with a vegetable peeler and reserve orange for another use. Tie peel, cinnamon stick, and cloves in cheesecloth. Combine all ingredients in a pot and simmer slowly for 20 minutes. Serve hot with ¼ cup rum added to each mug.

· · · · · · · ·

RASPBERRY LINZER COOKIES

Linzer dough is an Austrian specialty made from ground hazelnuts laced with cinnamon and cloves. It can be rolled to make many different pastries, including these attractive bakery-type cookies. Make as many as you like; leftover dough freezes very well and can be thawed overnight in the refrigerator, then rolled into other cookies or tarts. This dough needs to be rolled while it's very cold to prevent sticking.

Makes about 30

¼ pound shelled and skinned hazelnuts,
   toasted and cooled
½ cup plus 2 tablespoons sugar
2⅓ cups all-purpose flour
1½ teaspoons ground cinnamon
½ teaspoon ground cloves
¼ teaspoon baking powder
⅛ teaspoon salt
6 tablespoons unsalted butter, softened

66

1 egg
2 teaspoons grated lemon zest
½ teaspoon vanilla extract
¼ cup dry bread or cake crumbs
Approximately ¾ cup seedless raspberry
   jam for filling
Approximately ½ pound confectioners'
   sugar for dusting

1. Grind the hazelnuts in a food processor with 2 tablespoons sugar until a coarse meal results. Sift the flour, cinnamon, cloves, baking powder, and salt into a bowl. In another bowl, cream the butter and remaining sugar until mixture is pale yellow. Whip in the egg. Mixture should be fluffy. Add lemon zest, vanilla, nuts, and bread crumbs. Finally, fold in flour mixture. Form dough into two balls and chill until firm enough to roll.

2. To prepare cookies, preheat oven to 375°F. Remove one ball of dough from refrigerator and beat it with a rolling pin to flatten. Generously flour your work surface. Quickly roll out the dough into a sheet ⅛ inch thick (this dough must be worked with while cold). Cut out circles with a 2¼-inch scalloped-edge cookie cutter. Place circles on a cookie sheet. Repeat with second ball.

3. Using a 1-inch scalloped cutter, cut circles out of the center of half the cookies. If dough is sticky, chill before cutting out center circles. These will serve as the tops. Uncut cookies will be the bases. Rechill scrap dough, then roll again. Bake cookies for 9–10 minutes, until they turn golden brown. Do not overcook. Cool on cookie sheet for a couple of minutes, then remove to a rack.

4. To assemble cookies, spread 1 teaspoon raspberry jam on the center of a base piece, then place the top cookie over, pressing lightly to spread jam and adhere cookies. Decorate cookies by placing them on a wire rack and dusting with powdered sugar. Store in a sealed container in refrigerator.

. . . .

A CHARDONNAY TASTER

. . . .

Maryland Crab Cakes

Zucchini, Escarole, and Rice Minestra

Striped Bass Bundles with Leek Soubise and Wild Dill

Assorted Soft Cheeses

Sweet Grape Macédoine and Honey Puffed Pastry

. . . .

The Chardonnay grape finds its way into the great wines of the world, from the Chablis, Pouilly-Fuissés, and Montrachets of Burgundy to the outstanding selections produced in California. You may choose one of your favorite Chardonnays for this taster and serve it throughout or serve each course of this menu with its own unique wine.

MARYLAND CRAB CAKES

These crab cakes are best if made in advance and allowed to set in the refrigerator several hours before cooking. Make sure you don't fry them too quickly. They should sizzle easily in the butter and slowly become golden brown before being turned.

Serves 6

2 eggs, slightly beaten
⅓ cup mayonnaise
¼ cup chopped Italian (flat-leaf) parsley
1½ tablespoons chopped chives
1½ teaspoons Worcestershire sauce
1½ teaspoons Cajun-style seasoning or crab seasoning
1 teaspoon dry mustard
¼ teaspoon cayenne pepper
½ teaspoon salt or to taste
½ teaspoon freshly ground black pepper or to taste
1 cup soft fresh white bread crumbs
1½ pounds fresh crabmeat
½ cup cracker meal
⅓ cup or more unsalted butter
12 chive sprigs for garnish

1. In a medium-size bowl, combine egg, mayonnaise, parsley, chopped chives, Worcestershire sauce, Cajun seasoning, dry mustard, cayenne, salt, and pepper. Mix well and add bread crumbs. Toss. Gently fold in crabmeat. Shape mixture into 6

balls and flatten into cakes. Coat them with cracker meal on both sides. Place on a platter and chill until frying time, at least 1 hour.

2. In a large skillet, melt ⅓ cup butter over medium heat. Add crab cakes and panfry for about 4 minutes on each side or until golden brown, adding butter as necessary. Serve hot, each garnished with 2 crossed chive sprigs.

· · · · · · · ·

ZUCCHINI, ESCAROLE, AND RICE MINESTRA

The Italian minestra is a thick soup or porridge that is served in place of the pasta course before the meal's entrée. The Italians always serve up small portions, saving room for more to come. To them a cup of this hearty minestra is just right. For me, and probably you, it can serve as a one-dish meal. The recipe yields a large crock of soup. Just allow the leftovers to cool to room temperature, then freeze for another meal.

Serves about 12 (4 quarts)

¼ cup extra-virgin olive oil
1 medium-size onion, peeled and cut into medium dice
4 cloves garlic, peeled and minced
2–3 stalks celery, cut into medium dice, with some leaves
2 carrots, peeled and cut into medium dice
Leaves from ½ bunch Italian (flat-leaf) parsley, chopped coarse (about ½ cup)
4 small zucchini
3 small yellow summer squash
1 head escarole
1 14-ounce can chicken broth *or* 1¾ cups homemade

3 cups water
5 Roma-style (plum) tomatoes, peeled and seeded (see Index)
1 large sprig fresh thyme *or* ½ teaspoon dried
2 medium-size potatoes, peeled and diced medium
½ teaspoon salt plus additional to taste
⅓ cup Arborio (short-grain) rice
Leaves from ½ bunch fresh basil (about ¼ cup) *or* 2 tablespoons dried
1 teaspoon sugar
Freshly ground pepper to taste
1 tablespoon unsalted butter

1. Put 2 tablespoons of the oil in a large soup pot and heat over medium-high heat. Add onion, garlic, celery, and carrots. Stir well and add parsley. Sweat the vegetables for about 8 minutes, stirring occasionally. Cut zucchini and yellow squash into lengthwise quarters and then into medium dice. Add to soup pot.

2. Discard outer leaves of escarole. Make a few cuts from the root to the tips of the leaves, then squeeze tightly and slice across these cuts at about ½-inch intervals. Wash well under cold water and drain in a colander. Add to vegetables and turn up

heat. Sauté escarole until limp, then add chicken broth and water. Add tomatoes and thyme to the pot. Add potatoes and salt and bring to a simmer. Let simmer gently for 10 minutes, stirring frequently.

3. Turn off heat and remove thyme sprigs. Transfer about one-third of the vegetables from the soup to a food processor using a slotted spoon. Pulse machine to chop coarsely. Return vegetables to soup pot. Again, remove one-third of the vegetable mixture to a food processor and puree until smooth. Return to soup.

4. Bring to a simmer again and add rice. Simmer at low heat for 15 minutes, thinning with water if necessary. While soup is simmering, add the basil. Add sugar and season with salt and pepper to taste. Cook until rice is tender. Finish the minestra with the butter, allowing it to melt slowly as you stir. It should rest for 5 minutes before being served.

· · · · · · · ·

STRIPED BASS BUNDLES WITH LEEK SOUBISE AND WILD DILL

Striped bass come from many different waters to end up on our plates. They are preferred for this dish because they're both firm and delicate and come in a perfect size for bundling. If you can't find them, try any small whole fish fillets, about $\frac{1}{2}$ pound each, such as snapper, sole, or orange roughy (sections cut from large fillets will be difficult to use for bundles). A soubise is a classic French puree made from cooked onions and rice. This recipe uses leeks instead of onions for a softer taste—a tricky process, because white-fleshed fish are very subtle; one must take care not to overpower the refined flavor of the fish with too much accoutrement. Aromatic wild dill is quite different from the regular stuff and is worth searching for. You'll be happy to know you can prepare this casserole in advance and bake it when you want to.

Serves 6

LEEK SOUBISE
6 large leeks, white parts only
$\frac{1}{4}$ cup unsalted butter
1 clove garlic, peeled and minced
$\frac{1}{3}$ cup white rice
1 cup fish broth or bottled clam juice
$\frac{1}{2}$ teaspoon salt plus additional to taste
$\frac{1}{4}$ teaspoon freshly ground white pepper
    plus additional to taste
$\frac{1}{2}$ teaspoon sugar
1 teaspoon chopped wild dill

FISH
2 tablespoons unsalted butter, softened
Approximately 4 wild dill flowers *or*
    1 tablespoon chopped cultivated dill
6 8-ounce skinless fresh striped bass
    fillets
Salt to taste
$1\frac{1}{2}$ cups Chardonnay
Additional dill for garnishing

1. Begin by preparing the soubise. Split white parts of leeks in quarters lengthwise and slice ¼ inch thick. Place in a colander and wash several times under running water; they usually contain a lot of sand. Heat the ¼ cup butter over medium heat in a large saucepan. Add leeks and garlic. Slowly cook until tender, about 6 minutes. Add rice and sauté for a moment, then add broth, salt, pepper, sugar, and 1 teaspoon chopped dill. Allow to simmer, covered, until rice is tender, about 25 minutes.

2. Remove lid and turn heat up. Let excess moisture evaporate, stirring well and mashing lightly with a fork. Scrape it into a bowl and season to taste with salt and pepper. Allow to cool, then refrigerate.

3. Prepare an ovenproof 9″ × 13″ casserole dish by rubbing the bottom with softened butter. Arrange some flat wild dill flowers evenly over the bottom to cover.

4. To roll fish, lay them out on a work surface; the side where the skin used to be should be up. Sprinkle lightly with salt. Place a mound of the leek soubise, about 2 tablespoons, on each and spread it over the fillets. Roll up each fillet, starting at the smaller end, and arrange them on the dill in the casserole. Add the wine and cover with aluminum foil. The dish may be refrigerated all day at this point for later baking.

5. Preheat oven to 375°F. Bake covered casserole for 15 minutes. Remove from oven and check to see if the fish is cooked at the thickest part. Carefully remove fillets to a serving platter or plates. Remove the dill flowers and spoon sauce over top. Garnish with a sprig of dill.

· · · · · · · ·

ASSORTED SOFT CHEESES

I wouldn't be surprised to learn that the first person ever to try a bite of cheese followed it with a sip of wine—it's a combination appreciated for at least centuries. The delicate subtleties of Chardonnay wines should not be overpowered by sharp aged cheeses—soft unripened cheeses are far superior for a tasting, and the variety from which you may choose can be overwhelming. Almost every country in the world makes its own variation of cheese, some ready to eat in days after making, others taking almost a decade to age. For your Chardonnay party it's best to have a small assortment, depending on how many tasters there are. Your selection should include one of the quickly ripened, white-rind cheeses such as Brie or Camembert, so fresh that its center is still runny when cut. Another choice may be one of the chèvre cheeses, made with goat's milk and slightly more pungent than the white-rind cheeses. Many are sold plain, and others are marinated in olive oil, herbs, cracked pepper, or even black ash. My favorite is the Montrachet goat cheese that takes its name from the celebrated white burgundy produced in the same region of France. A third cheese to round out the taster might be a blue-veined variety, such as the Italian Gorgonzola,

French Roquefort, or English Stilton. Arrange your selection on a board and bring to room temperature well before serving. You may also add some apple slices or peeled pears around the cheeses and put a bunch or two of grapes on the board. With an assortment of crackers or breadsticks the cheeses should be served as long as there's wine to taste.

SWEET GRAPE MACEDOINE AND HONEY PUFFED PASTRY

'Tis the season of grapes, when they are sweetest and plumpest. Here they are poached in a spiced wine syrup, then sealed in a ramekin with a layer of puff pastry.

Serves 6

1 quart mixed Red Flame and white seedless grapes	2 cups Chardonnay
1½ cups sugar	2 cups water
1 cinnamon stick	1 pound frozen puff pastry, thawed in refrigerator overnight
6 cloves	1 egg, beaten with a pinch of salt
1 vanilla bean, split	⅓ cup honey
Zest of 1 lemon	

1. Remove grapes from stems. Wash in a colander and allow to drip dry. Divide them among six 10-ounce ramekins.

2. Combine sugar, cinnamon stick, cloves, vanilla bean, lemon zest, wine, and water in a saucepan. Bring to a simmer and simmer for 10 minutes. Remove from heat and strain into a bowl. Allow to cool, then refrigerate until chilled.

3. Lay thawed puff pastry on a floured surface and roll it evenly with a rolling pin until it's about ¼ inch thick. Using a round cutter or an inverted bowl, cut out six circles from the pastry; the diameter of each should be 1 inch wider than the diameter of your ramekins.

4. Divide chilled syrup among ramekins, filling them to within ½ inch from the top; use additional wine if necessary to stretch syrup. Wet the rims with water and lay a circle of pastry on each. Fold the borders down and seal them to the ramekins, wetting the dough underneath with water to form a tight seal. Cut a star pattern on the top of each with the tip of a sharp knife to provide vents. At this point they may be refrigerated overnight if desired.

5. To bake ramekins, preheat oven to 375°F. Paint the top of the pastry evenly with the egg wash. Bake for about 20 minutes, until pastry is browned and puffed. Meanwhile, heat honey in a small pot. Paint tops of pastries with the hot honey and serve immediately.

. . . .

OCTOBERFEAST

· · · · · · · ·

Boneless Chicken Thighs Stewed with Garlic and Sweet Fall Peppers

Warm Green Bean and Potato Salad

Cranberry Kuchen with Vanilla Bean Ice Cream

· · · · · · · ·

BONELESS CHICKEN THIGHS
STEWED WITH GARLIC AND SWEET FALL PEPPERS

The beauty of this dish depends on the variety of peppers you bring to it. Peppers are most abundant in October in California, and wonderful red, green, and even yellow bell peppers are available then at reasonable prices. If you prefer spicy flavors, add some jalapeños, but with caution—they can be very powerful.

Serves 4

2 red bell peppers
2 yellow or green bell peppers
1–2 jalapeño chilies, to taste (optional)
2 medium-size onions, peeled
6 boneless, skinless chicken thighs
Salt to taste
Freshly ground black pepper to taste

All-purpose flour for dusting chicken
½ cup olive oil
Leaves from ½ bunch Italian (flat-leaf) parsley, hopped (about ½ cup)
8 cloves garlic, peeled and chopped coarse
1 cup Italian white wine

1. Slice peppers through the stem and remove seeds. Quarter each half lengthwise. Cut onions in half crosswise, then into ½-inch lengthwise slices.

2. Cut chicken lengthwise into 3–4 strips. Salt and pepper strips and dust with flour. Heat ¼ cup of the olive oil in a large skillet until hot but not smoking. Fry chicken pieces on each side until light brown, keeping the oil hot. Remove to a large roasting pan or dutch oven. Discard oil from skillet.

3. Add remaining ¼ cup olive oil to skillet, heat until hot, then sauté onions until they begin to color. Add parsley, peppers, and garlic. Sauté until garlic begins to color; add wine and mix well. Sprinkle generously with salt and pepper. Arrange peppers and sauce evenly over chicken. Cover with foil. (Pan may be held at room temperature for up to 2 hours at this point until 30 minutes before serving time.)

4. Preheat oven to 400°F and bake chicken for 20–30 minutes. Remove foil and toss well. Preheat broiler and broil until peppers begin to crack and char. Serve immediately.

. . . .

WARM GREEN BEAN AND POTATO SALAD

This was one of my grandmother Til's secret preparations, and no one could ever perfectly duplicate her seasoning—she always used her fingertips to sprinkle everything. To the best of my recollection, this is what she did.

Serves 4

2 large baking potatoes
¼ cup extra-virgin olive oil plus 1
   tablespoon or to taste
2 cloves garlic, peeled and minced
1½ pounds fresh green beans, ends
   trimmed
½ teaspoon sugar
Salt to taste
Freshly ground black pepper to taste

1. Bring a large pot of salted water to a boil. Peel potatoes and cut them into 1-inch cubes. Put them in the pot of water. Bring to a boil, lower heat, and simmer for 8 minutes. Meanwhile, heat ¼ cup oil in a small pan and cook the garlic for several minutes, without browning, over very low heat.

2. Add green beans after potatoes have cooked for 8 minutes, bring to a boil, and cook for 5 minutes longer, until beans are tender.

3. Drain beans and potatoes in a colander, then return them to the pot. Add garlic and oil from small pan. Sprinkle with sugar, salt, pepper, and remaining olive oil to taste. Stir beans with a rubber spatula. Mash half of the potatoes lightly with a fork. Pour in a little water to keep the beans moist and mix well. Either serve immediately or transfer to a serving bowl, then reheat at dinnertime in the microwave. May be served at room temperature.

. . . .

CRANBERRY KUCHEN WITH VANILLA BEAN ICE CREAM

Cranberries come in late fall from great cranberry bogs off the shores of New England. At harvest time the fields are flooded and the berries float to the top. A special machine gathers them up, and we eventually find them in plastic bags at the market. We see them only for part of the year, so hide a couple of bags in the freezer—they'll keep there for months.

Serves 6

2 cups fresh cranberries, washed

STREUSEL TOPPING
¾ cup all-purpose flour
½ cup sugar
½ teaspoon ground cinnamon
3 tablespoons unsalted butter, softened

BATTER
1 egg
½ cup sugar
½ teaspoon ground cinnamon
½ cup milk
2 tablespoons vegetable oil
1 cup all-purpose flour
½ teaspoon salt
2 teaspoons baking powder

Vanilla Bean Ice Cream (recipe follows)

1. Preheat oven to 375°F and grease an 8-inch round cake pan. Place cranberries in a food processor and pulse until coarsely chopped. Set aside. Prepare streusel topping by combining flour, sugar, and cinnamon in a small bowl. Cut in butter until it's the size of small peas.

2. To make the batter, break egg into a bowl and add sugar, cinnamon, milk, and oil. Whisk well. Sift together flour, salt, and baking powder. Whisk into egg mixture and blend well. Pour into prepared pan. Arrange cranberries over batter and sprinkle evenly with streusel topping. Bake for 30 minutes. Serve warm with ice cream.

VANILLA BEAN ICE CREAM

Now's the time to make your favorite vanilla ice cream. Make sure you use real vanilla beans, split in half lengthwise, when you cook the cream. The tiny seeds inside the beans give the ice cream both a special flavor and a professional speckled appearance.

Makes 1 quart

1½ cups milk
2 vanilla beans
⅔ cup sugar
3 egg yolks
Pinch of salt
1 cup whipping cream
2 teaspoons vanilla extract

1. Heat milk in a large saucepan until simmering. Split the vanilla beans lengthwise and scrape out seeds with a spoon; add both seeds and beans to simmering milk. Add sugar and stir to dissolve.

2. In a bowl, beat egg yolks with a pinch of salt. Slowly stir about half of the hot milk into the eggs. Return egg yolk mixture to milk in saucepan. Cook over medium heat, stirring occasionally, until mixture thickens slightly and coats the back of a wooden spoon. Do not allow to boil. Remove from heat at once and pour through a strainer into a stainless-steel bowl. Add cream and vanilla extract. Chill thoroughly. Freeze in ice cream maker according to manufacturer's instructions.

· · · · · · · ·

AFTERNOON STEW

· · · · · · · ·

Mother's Stew with Potatoes and Vegetables

Basil Poppy Seed Dumplings

Spiced Plum Strudel

· · · · · · · ·

MOTHER'S STEW WITH POTATOES AND VEGETABLES

This recipe brings back memories of fall, when my mother would prepare this special one-dish meal, slowly cooked over the afternoon. Mom always made the stew with chunks of pork sirloin, and it's still my favorite meat, though you can, for variety, make a beef stew or even try it with lamb. Be sure to allow time for the piping-hot stew to rest for at least 15 minutes before serving so that the flavors will mellow. Never rush a stew.

Serves 4–5

2 pounds boneless pork, beef, or lamb
    stew meat
2 tablespoons vegetable oil
8 cloves garlic, peeled and sliced thin
1 large onion, peeled and diced
4 carrots, peeled and cut into 2-inch
    pieces
¼ cup ½-inch-thick sliced celery tips and
    leaves
1 14-ounce can beef broth
1 16-ounce can whole peeled tomatoes,
    including liquid

1 tablespoon fresh thyme leaves *or* 1
    teaspoon dried
Salt to taste
Freshly ground pepper to taste
Pinch of ground cloves
3 medium-size potatoes
approximately 1 cup (1 10-ounce
    package) frozen green peas
Approximately ½ cup water
Basil Poppy Seed Dumplings (recipe
    follows)

1. Trim fat from meat. Heat vegetable oil in a large heavy pot. Sear meat cubes in oil over high heat until brown on one side. Drain off liquids and fat, then continue to brown meat, stirring occasionally, for about 5 minutes.

2. Remove excess fat from pot and turn heat to medium-high. Add garlic, onions, carrots, and celery, stirring well. Continue to cook slowly until onions are nicely caramelized, about 10 minutes. Add beef broth, tomatoes, and thyme. Stir well and

lightly salt and pepper. Add a sprinkle of cloves. Cover and simmer slowly until meat is almost tender, about 1 hour. Break up tomatoes with a fork as they cook.

3. Meanwhile, peel potatoes and cut into 1-inch cubes; hold in water to prevent discoloration. When meat is almost tender, add potatoes, stirring well. Cover and continue to simmer for about 15 minutes more, stirring occasionally. Add peas and mash a few of the carrots and potatoes against the side of the pan with a fork, thickening the sauce. Add water to keep the sauce fairly thin. Bring stew to a simmer. Season with salt and pepper. Cook for 1 minute, turn off heat, and keep covered. Meanwhile, prepare Basil Poppy Seed Dumplings as directed. (If you don't want dumplings, cook the stew until potatoes are soft, stirring well. Serve with hot bread or biscuits.)

· · · · · · · ·

BASIL POPPY SEED DUMPLINGS

A good addition to the rich sauce of the stew, the basil in these dumplings gives them a special quality and freshness, and the poppy seeds add lightness and crunch.

2 cups all-purpose flour
1 teaspoon salt
4 teaspoons baking powder
1 tablespoon poppy seeds
Leaves from ½ bunch fresh basil (about ¼
  cup) *or* 2 tablespoons dried
⅔ cup milk
1 egg
2 tablespoons unsalted butter, melted
Additional unsalted butter

1. Combine flour, salt, baking powder, and poppy seeds in a bowl. Mix well. Mince basil leaves as fine as possible and add to flour, stirring well. In a separate bowl, combine milk and egg. Blend with a fork. Add egg mixture and melted butter to flour mixture, stirring with the fork until evenly moistened.

2. Season stew with salt and pepper as necessary. With your fingers, break apart walnut-size dumplings and arrange over surface of simmering stew. Fit as many as possible, but don't pack; leave vent holes. Simmer stew for 5 minutes without the cover, then cover and steam until dumplings are fully cooked, about 15 minutes more. Dot tops of dumplings with a few thin slices of additional butter. If stew seems too thick under dumplings, add water down the sides of pan and shake to incorporate. Allow stew and dumplings to rest for at least 15 minutes before serving.

· · · · · · · ·

SPICED PLUM STRUDEL

This strudel is made from phyllo, a type of dough purchased frozen in sheets that resemble tissue paper. Here it's carefully rolled with a filling and bakes into a flaky pastry bursting with purple plums and raisins. It is quite a bit of work, and you should make it only if you have a couple of hours to play in the kitchen. But oh, will your friends be happy!

Serves 15

2 pounds purple plums, stems removed
1 pound white raisins
3 cups sugar
4 teaspoons ground cinnamon
1½ teaspoons ground allspice
1 cup fine dry bread crumbs

½ teaspoon freshly grated nutmeg
1 1-pound box frozen phyllo dough, thawed according to package directions
1 pound unsalted butter, melted
Confectioners' sugar for sprinkling strudels

1. Cut plums in half, remove pit, and cut each half into three or four wedges. Place in a large bowl with raisins, 2 cups of the sugar, 3 teaspoons of the cinnamon, and ½ teaspoon of the allspice. Mix very well. In a separate bowl, combine bread crumbs, remaining 1 cup sugar, remaining teaspoon cinnamon, nutmeg, and remaining ½ teaspoon allspice.

2. Remove phyllo dough from package and unroll flat on counter. Cover immediately with a sheet of plastic wrap.

3. Working rapidly, remove a single sheet of phyllo from under plastic; re-cover. Paint sheet lightly with melted butter. Sprinkle evenly with 1 heaped tablespoon of the bread crumb mixture. Cover with another sheet of phyllo and repeat process. Proceed rapidly until you have finished six layers, buttering the top sheet as well and sprinkling with crumbs.

4. Preheat oven to 400°F. Arrange one-third of the plum filling in a log shape across the bottom (long end) of the phyllo, leaving a 2-inch border on the bottom and sides. Roll bottom edge of pastry over filling one time, then fold in sides, continuing to roll carefully to form a log. Make sure sides are closed. Place on a large baking sheet, seam down, and paint with butter. Repeat with remaining phyllo and filling to form two additional logs. Place all three logs on the same large baking sheet and bake for 40 minutes or until glistening brown.

5. Allow to cool for 5 minutes, then remove carefully to a cooling rack using two spatulas. The strudels should sit for at least 30 minutes before being cut (or refrigerate them overnight, wrapped lightly in foil). To serve strudels, sprinkle generously with powdered sugar and slice with a large serrated knife on the bias. You should get about five slices per log.

· · · · · · · ·

INDIAN SUMMER

· · · · · · · ·

Puree of Pumpkin Soup with Parsley Pesto

Roasted Loin of Pork with Wild Rice and Corn Stuffing

Pecan-Raisin Baked Apples

Indian Pudding

· · · · · · · ·

Each fall, when there is that brief warm spell that marks the last time we'll be able to get a tan before the sleet and snow set in, we doff our mackinaws in favor of light sweaters and windbreakers and enjoy the last few days of driving with the top down. Here's a menu that uses some of the foods of the season.

PUREE OF PUMPKIN SOUP WITH PARSLEY PESTO

All sorts of winter squashes can be used for this soup, though pumpkin will give you a special bright orange color. Served with a bit of the green pesto across the top, it makes for an attractive and savory autumn soup. As with most pureed soups, this may be prepared ahead of time and reheated.

Serves 6–8

¼ cup unsalted butter
2 cups chopped onion
1 carrot, peeled and chopped
1 quart chicken broth, preferably homemade (as in Grandma's Cappelletti Soup; see Index)
1 large apple, peeled, cored, and chopped
2 pounds peeled and cut-up fresh pumpkin in 1-inch chunks (about 1 4-pound pumpkin)

1¼ cups apple juice
1 cup half-and-half
Salt to taste
Freshly ground white pepper to taste
¼ teaspoon freshly grated nutmeg or to taste
Parsley Pesto (recipe follows)

1. Melt the butter in a large pot. Add onions and cook over low heat until soft, 15–20 minutes. Do not allow to brown. Add carrots halfway through the cooking.

2. Add broth to onions along with apples and pumpkin. Cook over medium-low heat, partially covered, until very tender, about 35–40 minutes.

3. Strain soup through a strainer, reserving liquid, and puree the solids in a food processor until smooth, adding some of the cooking liquid to thin it out. Return all cooking liquid, puree, and apple juice to the pot and simmer until it's the desired consistency. Add half-and-half and season with salt, pepper, and nutmeg. Ladle into soup bowls and garnish with Parsley Pesto.

PARSLEY PESTO

1 cup Italian (flat-leaf) parsley leaves
1 clove garlic, peeled
¼ cup pine nuts or shelled walnuts,
    toasted
½ cup extra-virgin olive oil
Salt to taste
Freshly ground black pepper to taste
½ cup grated Parmesan cheese
1 tablespoon unsalted butter, softened

1. Wash parsley leaves and dry well. Place them in a food processor along with garlic, pine nuts, and olive oil. Puree until smooth, scraping sides of bowl. Add salt and pepper to taste.

2. Remove pesto to a small bowl and stir in Parmesan and butter until smooth. Add a little water if it seems too thick. Spoon a line of pesto across the top of the hot soup before serving.

· · · · · · · ·

ROASTED LOIN OF PORK
WITH WILD RICE AND CORN STUFFING

In a restaurant roasting and serving a whole loin of pork is not particularly difficult. The meat is simply roasted ahead of time, and big, double-boned chops are sliced off and served. At home it can be a lot of work, especially at dinnertime. To make life easier and just as tasty, I've given the recipe as a stuffed, double-ribbed loin chop. The corn and wild rice stuffing also can be served as a marvelous side dish for any roasted or grilled meat, fish, or poultry. Simply bake it in a casserole, covered with foil, for about 20 minutes.

Serves 6

¼ pound wild rice
2 quarts water
1½ cups fresh or frozen corn kernels
1 small red bell pepper, cut into ¼-inch dice
1 cup coarsely chopped dry white bread crumbs

¼ cup chopped cilantro or Italian (flat-leaf) parsley
⅓ cup meat or chicken broth
¼ cup unsalted butter, melted
Salt to taste
Freshly ground black pepper to taste
6 double-rib center loin pork chops

1. Prepare stuffing by boiling wild rice in 2 quarts salted water until tender, about 50 minutes. About 5 minutes before it's cooked, add the corn and diced peppers to the boiling rice. Drain in a colander when finished. Transfer to a large bowl and add bread crumbs, cilantro, broth, and melted butter. Toss and season with salt and pepper.

2. Preheat oven to 350°F. To make the stuffing pocket in the pork chops, insert a boning knife between the two ribs of the chop and saw back and forth inside the meat, cutting a large pocket inside the meat but making only a 1-inch opening between the bones. Be careful not to cut through to the other side. The stuffing is inserted into the chop from this small opening between the bones, not from the meat side; thus there is no need to bind the stuffed chops with twine, since it will not ooze out between the bones. Stuff each chop with several spoonfuls of stuffing, forcing it into the pocket until the chop is plump.

3. Season the chops with salt and pepper. Arrange chops, rib down and fat up, in a baking pan and roast for about 1½ hours or until tender. Allow to rest for 10 minutes before serving. Spoon any juices that have accumulated in the pan over each before serving.

. . . .

PECAN-RAISIN BAKED APPLES

Baked apples seemed to be a common side dish years ago, and we've forgotten how tasty they really can be. You can stuff them with all sorts of dried fruit and nut combinations, complementing roasted pork perhaps better than anything.

Serves 6

6 large baking apples
1 cup dark brown sugar
1 cup water
2 tablespoons unsalted butter
½ teaspoon ground cinnamon
½ teaspoon freshly grated nutmeg
½ cup raisins
½ cup chopped pecans, toasted

1. Preheat oven to 350°F. Cut off the top of each apple and cut out core. Pare a strip around the "belly" of each and place them in a baking dish.

2. Prepare syrup by combining brown sugar, water, butter, cinnamon, and nutmeg. Bring to a boil and cook for 5 minutes. Remove from heat.

3. Mix raisins and pecans in a small bowl. Divide mixture among the cavities in the apples. Pour hot syrup over apples and bake for 45 minutes to 1 hour, until apples are soft, basting occasionally while baking. Serve hot.

· · · · · · · ·

INDIAN PUDDING

Many years ago, when the cozy old cookstove was used to heat the kitchen, an Indian pudding could most likely be found sitting in the oven. It was an inexpensive dessert and could be set in a warm oven to bake through the hours of the day. Serve with heavy cream or ice cream.

Serves 6

½ cup white or yellow cornmeal
3 cups milk, scalded
⅔ cup dark molasses
½ teaspoon ground cinnamon
½ teaspoon freshly grated nutmeg
½ teaspoon ground ginger
½ teaspoon salt
2 tablespoons unsalted butter
½ cup hot milk

1. Preheat oven to 300°F. Sprinkle cornmeal into scalded milk and stir with a whisk. Cook, stirring, until mixture bubbles. Continue for 5 minutes, stirring constantly. Remove from heat. Stir in molasses, spices, and salt.

2. Use 2 tablespoons butter to grease a terra-cotta baking dish or 1½-quart ovenproof casserole. Pour cornmeal mixture into dish and add ½ cup hot milk. Stir gently. Bake for 2–2½ hours. Serve with simple heavy cream or vanilla ice cream while still warm.

· · · · · · · ·

W I N T E R

Winter is the season that freezes your toes and excites your nose. As the mercury drops and the nights grow raw, the food becomes heartier and the drinks stronger. Enhance the mood with exuberant fare, from steaming stews to oven-roasted meals.

A COZY WINTER GATHERING

· · · · · · · ·

Watercress and Red Onion Salad with Balsamic Vinaigrette

Oven-Roasted Herbed Meat Loaf

Glazed Root Vegetables

White Chocolate Cake Soufflés with Tangerine Sauce

· · · · · · · ·

WATERCRESS AND RED ONION SALAD
WITH BALSAMIC VINAIGRETTE

The best watercress is harvested in winter. Sweet red onions contrast with its fresh bite while a little added romaine, also of exceptional quality in winter, acts as a neutral green. The secret to this salad, as with all salads, is to chill the greens so they crisp, tossing them with the dressing at the last possible moment.

Serves 4

3 bunches fresh watercress
1 small head romaine lettuce
1 small red onion
½ cup chopped walnuts, toasted
Balsamic Vinaigrette (recipe follows)

1. Well before serving, pinch tender tips off watercress and remove bottom leaves from stems. Place the greens in a colander. Trim the outer leaves of the romaine and cut off dark green tips. Make two cuts lengthwise toward the root, then cut across the head to make ½-inch slices. Wash this and the watercress together with lots of cold water. Drain and dry gently with paper towels or whirl in salad spinner. Refrigerate for at least 1 hour to crisp.

2. To serve salad, peel onion and trim off root and stem. Cut onion in half through the root. Lay it on its side, then slice as thinly as you can. Place the greens in a mixing bowl and sprinkle with walnuts and onion. Pour about ¼ cup of the vinaigrette over and toss. Add dressing as necessary. Serve on chilled salad plates.

BALSAMIC VINAIGRETTE

Balsamic vinegar is made mostly in Italy by a special process that gives this vinegar a unique woody flavor. It has recently become popular across America and makes one of the finest salad vinegars I know. At the restaurant we go through gallons of it a week. You may want to double this recipe since it keeps in the refrigerator for up to a month. It is a powerful vinaigrette, so add it to the salad with reserve—you can always add more.

Makes about 2 cups

2 tablespoons seasoned rice wine vinegar
2 teaspoons Dijon mustard
4 dashes of Tabasco sauce
3 teaspoons sugar
1 teaspoon dried oregano
6 tablespoons balsamic vinegar
5 cloves garlic, peeled
1 teaspoon freshly ground black pepper
1 teaspoon Worcestershire sauce
1½ teaspoons salt
1 cup extra-virgin olive oil

Combine all ingredients except oil in a blender until smooth. While blender is running, pour in oil. The dressing is best if flavors are allowed to mellow for a day or two before serving.

· · · · · · · ·

OVEN-ROASTED HERBED MEAT LOAF

Using the oven on cold winter nights warms the house with savory aromas that tease and tantalize throughout the evening. Kitchen window panes become steamy as this flavorful meat loaf, laced with fresh herbs, onion, and garlic, roasts in the oven. The vegetables cook in the oven as well, making this an ideal choice for a dinner party, since you can do most of the cleanup *before* guests arrive. The recipe easily feeds eight people—leftovers make an extraordinary sandwich the next day. The pork is added to keep the meat loaf moist and to add flavor. If you don't like spicy food, use a sweet red or green pepper instead of the chilies. Early in the day or the day before is the best time to prepare the meat loaf, then refrigerate it until the appropriate cooking time. Remember, it must sit for 15 minutes after cooking so it can plump and reabsorb its cooking juices.

Serves 8

Leaves from 1 bunch Italian (flat-leaf) parsley (about 1 cup packed)

Leaves from ½ bunch fresh thyme (about ¼ cup)

Leaves from 1 bunch fresh basil (about ½ cup packed)

¼ loaf day-old French bread

2¼ pounds lean freshly ground beef (not frozen)

1½ pounds lean ground pork

1 medium-size onion, peeled and cut into small dice

5 cloves garlic, peeled and minced very fine (or put through a garlic press)

3 eggs

⅓ cup ketchup

10 dashes of Worcestershire sauce

¼ cup grated Parmesan cheese

1 tablespoon salt or to taste

½ tablespoon freshly ground black pepper or to taste

1–2 fresh hot red and/or green chilies *or* red and green bell peppers, to taste

Fresh herb sprigs for garnish

1. Put the herb leaves in a food processor and process until lightly chopped. Break off pieces of bread and add to the food processor, pulsing until bread is crumbed.

2. Put all remaining ingredients except chilies, including bread crumb mixture, in a very large bowl. Mix the meat loaf thoroughly, using a large carving fork to keep it light. It is important that the meat loaf be seasoned properly, so fry a small patty in a skillet to taste for the correct amount of salt and pepper.

3. Cut the chilies or bell peppers into thin slices. Oil the bottom and sides of an oval 1-gallon roasting pan or casserole. Arrange chili slices on bottom of pan. Pat some of the meat loaf mixture on top of the chilies, being careful not to move the arranged peppers, and press down. Continue to fill pan, pressing firmly and smoothing top of meat loaf. (Meat loaf may be refrigerated overnight until ready to bake.)

4. Preheat the oven to 350°F and bake, uncovered, for 1½ hours or until a meat thermometer registers 160°F directly at the midpoint of the meat loaf. Remove and allow to cool for 15 minutes. Siphon off remaining juices and fat. Place a serving platter on top of meat loaf pan and, holding it with two hands, flip the meat loaf over onto platter. Arrange Glazed Root Vegetables (recipe follows) around meat loaf and garnish with a few herb sprigs.

. . . .

GLAZED ROOT VEGETABLES

Serves 4

1 rutabaga, peeled
2 turnips
1 large onion, peeled
3 carrots
3 parsnips
¼ cup unsalted butter
Salt to taste
Freshly ground black pepper to taste
¼ cup packed dark brown sugar

1. Preheat oven to 425°F. Cut rutabagas, turnips, and onions into uniform wedges about the size of a tomato wedge. Cut carrots and parsnips into thirds on the bias. Put the butter into a shallow 2- or 3-quart ovenproof dish and place in oven to melt. When melted, add vegetables, sprinkle generously with salt and pepper, and sprinkle with sugar. Toss well.

2. Roast for 30 minutes. (Meanwhile, you may prepare the meat loaf.) Lower heat to 350°F and continue cooking vegetables, tossing often, for 1½ hours more, depending on size of vegetables. They should be soft and golden brown, with a light glaze. When finished, tent with foil and keep warm until serving time.

. . . .

WHITE CHOCOLATE CAKE SOUFFLES WITH TANGERINE SAUCE

These soufflés, which have a particularly cakelike consistency, are a dazzling finale to a dinner party. Though they do require last-minute baking, with a little practice they take almost no time at all. Make sure you butter the ramekins all the way up the sides; if not, the rising soufflé may catch on an unbuttered area and puff up unevenly. The tangerine sauce can be prepared while the soufflés cook.

Serves 4 (1 cup sauce)

SOUFFLES
3 tablespoons unsalted butter, softened
¼ pound white chocolate
2 tablespoons milk
5½ tablespoons sugar plus additional for
   sprinkling ramekins
3 egg yolks
1 teaspoon vanilla extract
4 egg whites
Confectioners' sugar for dusting

TANGERINE SAUCE
¾ cup tangerine juice
2 teaspoons Triple Sec
2 tablespoons sugar
2 teaspoons cornstarch
½ cup tangerine sections, chopped

1. Preheat oven to 350°F. To prepare the soufflés, thoroughly rub the butter over the sides and bottoms of each of four 8-ounce soufflé ramekins and sprinkle with a little additional sugar, tilting to coat the sides. Be sure you don't miss any spots.

2. Melt the chocolate in the top of a double boiler and stir in milk and ¼ cup sugar, mixing well. Remove from heat and allow to cool for 5 minutes. Add the egg yolks, beating constantly. Stir in vanilla.

3. Whip the egg whites together until they form stiff peaks, adding remaining 1½ tablespoons sugar halfway through. Stir one-third of the whites into the yolks, then fold in remaining whites until incorporated. Fill each ramekin almost to the brim with the soufflé mixture and bake in the center of the oven until puffed and browned, about 15 minutes.

4. While soufflés are baking, prepare Tangerine Sauce: Combine tangerine juice, Triple Sec, sugar, and cornstarch in a small saucepan. Simmer, stirring constantly for 4 minutes. Add tangerine pieces.

5. When soufflés are ready, remove from oven and sprinkle with confectioners' sugar. Make a hole in center of each soufflé and spoon in a little hot Tangerine Sauce, serving additional sauce in a sauceboat.

. . . .

SUPER BOWL SUNDAY

....

Chicken Chili and Assorted Condiments

Super Bowl Brownies

....

CHICKEN CHILI AND ASSORTED CONDIMENTS

To the many people who asked for Indigo's Chicken Chili recipe, here it is. We make hundreds of pounds of this a week at the restaurant and can still run out of it on those cold chili kind of evenings. The key to this chili is the chicken—choose top-quality poultry, preferably free-range. Unlike its beef counterpart, chicken chili need not stew for several hours. It doesn't keep in the refrigerator for more than a couple of days, but it freezes well for quite a long time. For the Super Bowl you can make it the day before and reheat it for the game. At the restaurant we top each bowl with a handful of chopped red onions, melt some cheddar cheese on it, stick it with a few fried blue corn tortilla chips, and garnish with cilantro sprigs. Your choice of condiments can include these and others, such as sour cream, roasted corn, green chilies, and crackers.

Makes 2 gallons, serving 10–12

¾ pound dried small red beans, such as pinto beans
2 quarts water
6 tablespoons olive oil
2 large onions, peeled and diced
½ cup peeled cloves garlic
8 small jalapeño chilies, minced fine
48 ounces canned stewed tomatoes, including liquid
5–6 bay leaves
1 12-ounce bottle beer
¼ cup ground cumin
¼ cup dried oregano
¼ cup mild chili powder
3 tablespoons Hungarian paprika
1 tablespoon unsweetened cocoa powder
½ teaspoon ground cinnamon
5 pounds boneless chicken thighs, skinned and cut into ¾-inch pieces
4 pounds boneless chicken thighs, skinned and ground coarse
½ cup yellow cornmeal
¼ cup salt or to taste

1. Rinse beans and set them to boil in the water for about 1½ hours. When tender, remove from heat and allow to rest in their cooking liquid; do not drain.

2. In a large kettle, heat oil and add onions. Cook for about 10 minutes over medium heat, until onions are tender and translucent. Add garlic and jalapeños to the onions. Cook for an additional few minutes.

3. Add stewed tomatoes, bay leaves, beer, cumin, oregano, chili powder, paprika, cocoa, and cinnamon. Bring to a boil and add all chicken meat. Stir well and simmer for about 30 minutes, uncovered, just until chicken is cooked.

4. Add beans and 1 cup of their cooking liquid to the chili. Bring to a simmer again. Stirring constantly, sprinkle the chili with a spoon of the cornmeal, stir it in, then repeat with remaining cornmeal, being careful not to create lumps. Simmer for a few more minutes; if the chili is too thick, add some more bean liquid or water. Season with salt. Remove bay leaves before serving. Serve hot.

· · · · · · · · ·

SUPER BOWL BROWNIES

Several years ago I toyed with the idea of selling brownies commercially. In preparation for this I began baking brownies by the gross, constantly adjusting the ingredients and the method in which they were assembled, in search of the perfect brownie. I found that using cocoa powder instead of melted chocolate gave them a unique chocolate flavor that I liked. I also found that my brownie was so rich it maintained a perfect fudgy consistency if eaten directly from the refrigerator. Although I scrapped the idea of selling them (probably because I was gaining so much weight eating the prototypes), what I ended up with was a recipe for rich, glorious brownies, laced with pecans—just the thing after a bowl of the spicy chicken chili on Super Bowl Sunday.

Makes 36 small or 24 large brownies

1 cup all-purpose flour
½ teaspoon salt
¾ cup unsweetened cocoa powder
2 cups (1 pound) unsalted butter,
  softened
3 cups sugar
3 eggs
2 tablespoons vanilla extract
1½ cups chopped pecans

1. Preheat oven to 350°F. Line a 16″ × 10″ × 1″ baking sheet with a sheet of heavy-duty aluminum foil cut about 4 inches larger than the pan. Fold edges of foil to make a 2-inch rim standing up on all four sides; the brownies puff up as they bake, and the rim prevents spills.

2. Sift flour, salt, and cocoa together. In a large mixing bowl, cream the butter and sugar until light and fluffy. Turn beater to low speed and add eggs, one at a time. Add vanilla. Turn off mixer and add flour/cocoa mixture all at once. Blend by hand with a spatula just until ingredients are combined, scraping sides of bowl. Stir in the pecans. Batter should be very thick.

3. Transfer batter to prepared pan and spread it to the sides using a spatula. (Running the spatula under hot water will prevent sticking.) Smooth evenly and bake for 25–28 minutes. Check the center of the brownies; when they are just barely set, remove the pan from the oven. Allow to cool to room temperature, then refrigerate until firm.

4. Remove brownies from refrigerator and invert onto a cutting surface. Peel off foil and cut into squares. Serve them chilled from the refrigerator. May be frozen for months.

· · · · · · · ·

CARNIVAL

. . . .

Iced Absolut Oysters

Muffaletta Pouch Bread Sandwiches with Marinated Olive Relish

Sweet Potato Chips

Bread Pudding and Whiskey Sauce

. . . .

Is there any more festive time of the year than Mardi Gras? This menu reflects New Orleans, the most partying town in the United States. If you've never been to Mardi Gras, there is no way to adequately describe the madness that takes place for the two weeks before the 40 days of Lent set in. If you can't get there, prepare this menu. It's not the same as being in the Crescent City, but it might give you some idea of what's being quaffed and supped down there.

ICED ABSOLUT OYSTERS

Fresh-shucked raw oysters are as much a part of the Mardi Gras celebration as anything, and they are in greatest abundance and at their plumpest during the winter. Felix's Oyster Bar in New Orleans is where the bivalve has been elevated to the status of a divinity. Patrons wait in line for a chance to sit at the bar and down a dozen— raw, of course, with perhaps a bit of cocktail sauce and maybe a splash of vodka.

Serves 6

24 fresh oysters	5 dashes of Tabasco sauce
¾ cup ketchup	Approximately 1½ cups Absolut vodka,
1½ teaspoons prepared horseradish	chilled in freezer
1½ teaspoons fresh lemon juice	Italian (flat-leaf) parsley for garnish

1. Wash outside of oyster shells with cold water. Open each with an oyster knife by inserting the tip into the base of the shell and twisting. Leave oyster in its half shell and arrange them on ice.

2. Prepare cocktail sauce by stirring together ketchup, horseradish, lemon juice, and Tabasco.

3. Fill each oyster to the top of the shell with chilled vodka and add a small spoonful of the cocktail sauce. Garnish with a small parsley leaf and serve.

. . . .

MUFFALETTA POUCH BREAD SANDWICHES WITH MARINATED OLIVE RELISH

No one in New Orleans can agree on who makes the best muffaletta sandwich. Traditionally a variety of cold cuts and cheeses packed in bread with a pungent, oily, marinated olive relish, they are decadent and almost too thick to bite into. My favorite muffaletta maker in New Orleans serves them up in homemade pouch bread, similar to pita. I especially like this version since it helps hold everything in place as you wrestle to eat your sandwich. In lieu of homemade bread, buy large pita-style pouch breads for your sandwiches. Make the olive relish the day before so the robust flavors can marinate.

Serves 6 (2 cups relish)

OLIVE RELISH
1 large red bell pepper
1 7-ounce jar pimiento-stuffed green olives
1 6-ounce can pitted ripe black olives
3 large cloves garlic, peeled and crushed
1 cup olive oil
¼ cup finely chopped Italian (flat-leaf) parsley leaves
2 tablespoons white wine vinegar

SANDWICHES
6 large pita breads
½ pound Italian salami, sliced
½ pound mild white cheese, such as Muenster, sliced
½ pound domestic (mild) provolone, sliced
½ pound mortadella, sliced

1. To make the relish, char the skin of the pepper over a gas flame or under a preheated broiler until black. Allow to sit for several minutes, then peel off black skin, rinsing your fingertips, not the pepper, under cold water. Coarsely chop the pepper.

2. Coarsely chop the green and black olives together in a food processor and place in a bowl. Add red peppers, garlic, olive oil, parsley, and vinegar. Mix well and let stand in refrigerator overnight.

3. To assemble sandwiches, cut a 3-inch opening into each pita bread. Spoon a little of the oil from the Olive Relish over the insides of each. Arrange the sandwich ingredients inside the pockets in this order: salami, Olive Relish, mild cheese, provolone, mortadella, and a bit more Olive Relish. Serve with Sweet Potato Chips (recipe follows).

. . . .

SWEET POTATO CHIPS

Here's a simple sweet twist to regular potato chips. If sweet potatoes aren't available, you can substitute yams, which are deeper in color and have ends that sort of come to a point. For crispy chips, make sure the oil stays hot while frying by not frying too many at a time.

Serves 6

3–4 medium-size sweet potatoes
Vegetable oil for frying
Salt to taste

1. Scrub the potatoes clean. Slice them very thin with a large very sharp knife. Place the slices in a large bowl of ice water. Soak in the refrigerator for at least 2 hours. When ready to cook, drain and dry potatoes thoroughly on paper towels.

2. Heat about 2 inches of vegetable oil in a large saucepan until hot, about 375°F. Fry in batches and cook quickly over medium-high heat. As they crisp and become slightly brown, remove them to a large bowl lined with paper towels. Repeat with remaining chips, making sure the temperature of the oil remains at 375°F. If the oil cools too much, the chips will not get crisp. Remove towels from bowl and toss chips with salt. Keep them uncovered, in a warm oven, until serving time.

. . . .

BREAD PUDDING AND WHISKEY SAUCE

No mention of the cuisine of New Orleans is complete without bread pudding. Hundreds of versions have been logged over the years, and this is my favorite. The lively sauce makes the difference. It must have a strong whiskey kick and should be served warm over the pudding.

Serves 12

1 French bread baguette, 1½ feet long
1 quart milk
3 eggs
2 cups sugar
2 tablespoons vanilla extract
1 teaspoon ground cinnamon
1 cup dark or golden raisins
3 tablespoons unsalted butter, melted

1. In a large bowl, break the bread into bite-size pieces. Pour milk over bread, toss, and allow to soak for 1 hour. Mix well.

2. Preheat oven to 375°F. Beat eggs with sugar. Stir in vanilla and cinnamon. Add to bread mixture along with raisins and mix well with a spoon.

3. Pour melted butter into a 13″ × 9″ × 2″ baking dish and tilt to coat evenly, including the sides. Pour in pudding and bake for 1 hour or until a knife inserted in the center comes out completely clean. May be refrigerated for several days. Serve warm or at room temperature.

WHISKEY SAUCE
Makes 2 cups

½ cup (¼ pound) unsalted butter
1 cup sugar
1 egg
¼ cup bourbon

Melt the butter and sugar together in the top of a double boiler. Beat the egg in a small bowl, then gradually whisk it into the butter. Remove from heat and cool slightly. Whisk in whiskey and keep warm over water until serving time. Pass with the pudding.

· · · · · · · ·

WONDERLAND

········

Lydia's Whole Baked Artichokes

Rosemary Chicken Strips and Fettuccine
with Sun-Dried Tomato and Garlic Cream

Pink Gingered Pear Compote with Cassis

········

LYDIA'S WHOLE BAKED ARTICHOKES

My friend Lydia Shire is one of the best chefs in the world. She made her reputation in Boston, came to Los Angeles and established herself here, then decided to return to Boston, where she opened her own fabulous restaurant. She makes extraordinary dishes, and one of my favorites is her recipe for artichokes. Thanks, Lydia!

Serves 4

4 large globe artichokes
5 cloves garlic, peeled
2 tablespoons drained capers
6 canned anchovy fillets, rinsed under water

¼ cup Italian (flat-leaf) parsley leaves
⅓ cup extra-virgin olive oil
1 cup or more water
¼ teaspoon freshly ground black pepper

1. Remove a few of the outer leaves from the artichokes. Cut off stems at base so artichokes will sit flat in roasting pan. Cut a 1-inch slice off tops as well. Set aside.

2. Finely chop together the garlic, capers, anchovies, and parsley. Pour the olive oil into a medium-size saucepan and add chopped garlic mixture. Cook over medium-high heat for a minute or 2, then add water and black pepper. Boil and reduce liquid by one-third.

3. Preheat oven to 350°F. Stand up artichokes in a roasting pan just large enough to contain them and pour reduced broth over them. Cover and bake until tender, about 1 hour, basting occasionally. Add more water as necessary to prevent them from drying out. Serve hot or at room temperature.

········

ROSEMARY CHICKEN STRIPS AND FETTUCCINE WITH SUN-DRIED TOMATO AND GARLIC CREAM

This delicious combination of flavors has been very popular at the restaurant. Sun-dried tomatoes must be reconstituted before use, and there are several ways to accomplish this. The best is simply to boil enough water to cover the dried tomatoes. Once boiling, add the tomatoes, stir, and immediately drain in a colander. Allow to stand for five minutes, then cut into julienne strips. The tomatoes can be used immediately or stored covered with olive oil in a jar in the refrigerator indefinitely. It's important not to let this pasta sauce become too thick, remembering that it will continue to thicken even as you eat.

Serves 4

2 tablespoons olive oil
2 boneless chicken breast halves, skinned and cut into ½-inch strips
4–5 cloves garlic, peeled and sliced thin or minced
10 sun-dried tomatoes, plumped in water and sliced thin
1 quart half-and-half
1 chicken bouillon cube, preferably Knorr-Swiss brand

2 teaspoons finely chopped fresh rosemary *or* 1 teaspoon dried
Salt to taste
Freshly ground black pepper to taste
1 pound dried fettuccine or other shape dried pasta
1 heaped tablespoon grated Parmesan cheese

1. Boil salted water for pasta. In a large saucepan, heat olive oil over medium-high heat. Add chicken and sauté quickly to sear. When chicken is lightly browned, reduce heat and add garlic and sun-dried tomatoes. Sauté for a moment, until garlic is beginning to color. Add half-and-half, bouillon cube, and rosemary. Scrape the bottom of the skillet with a wooden spoon, stirring well. Simmer until sauce has thickened to heavy cream consistency and no more, about 5 minutes. Add salt and pepper. Cover and turn off heat.

2. Cook pasta as directed in "Dried Pasta" (see Index). Drain and add to sauce. Turn heat to low and move fettuccine around in the sauce, taking care not to tangle the noodles. Heat for a minute or 2 until the pasta absorbs some of the sauce and the sauce thickens slightly. If it becomes too thick, thin with additional milk. Keep it on the thin side. Add Parmesan while stirring. Serve immediately.

• • • • • • • •

PINK GINGERED PEAR COMPOTE WITH CASSIS

Serve these sparkling pears in a clear glass serving bowl. The longer the fruit sits in the syrup, the better the flavor. If you're lucky enough to come across fresh quinces, substitute them for the pears.

Serves 4

½ cup sugar
1 bottle fruity white wine, such as
   Gerwürztraminer or Riesling
¾ cup crème de cassis
1 cinnamon stick, broken into pieces
6 cloves
½ tablespoon black peppercorns
1 3-inch piece of fresh gingerroot, peeled
   and halved
1 lemon, sliced
4 large Bosc pears

1. Combine sugar, wine, cassis, cinnamon, cloves, peppercorns, ginger, and lemon in a medium-size saucepan and bring to a simmer.

2. Peel the pears, slice in half lengthwise, and core. Add to the saucepan. Poach the pears for 25–30 minutes, until slightly translucent and just tender.

3. Remove the saucepan from the heat. Allow pears to cool in the syrup. Transfer pears and syrup to a serving bowl; leave spices in syrup. Refrigerate overnight. Serve pears chilled.

. . . .

A COUNTRY SUPPER

·······

Shredded Romaine and Sweet Onion Salad
with Chèvre and Roasted Chestnuts

Chicken Giblet Stew with Tiny Sausage Meatballs and Fresh Peas

Wild Mushroom Polenta

Grandma's Boiled Cake with Hot Buttered Rum Sauce

········

SHREDDED ROMAINE AND SWEET ONION SALAD
WITH CHEVRE AND ROASTED CHESTNUTS

This salad demands crisp, firm romaine, which is at the height of its season in winter. Tearing or cutting lettuces in different ways can drastically affect the outcome of a salad. For a Caesar salad the romaine is torn into large pieces. For this special little salad you must shred the lettuce and toss it with sweet onions, goat cheese, and roasted chestnuts.

Serves 4

16 large chestnuts
1 teaspoon extra-virgin olive oil
1 head romaine lettuce
1 red onion, peeled

5 ounces goat cheese, preferably Montrachet
¼ cup Balsamic Vinaigrette (see Index) or your favorite vinaigrette

1. Preheat oven to 425°F. Cut a small slit along the side of each chestnut with the tip of a paring knife to prevent bursting in oven. Roast for 15 minutes. Allow to rest for 10 minutes, then peel the shells and skins from each. Break into pieces. Toss with olive oil and set aside.

2. Trim the outer leaves from the romaine and cut off tips. Make several slices lengthwise through the head, then gather it together and cut crosswise into ¼-inch slices, julienning the lettuce. Wash in cold water and spin dry in a salad spinner; place in a bowl. Cut onion in half, lay flat, and slice as thin as you can. Arrange on top of lettuce. Chill.

3. To serve, crumble the cheese on the lettuce and drizzle modestly with dressing. Toss, breaking up lumps of cheese, and add more dressing as necessary. Arrange on plates. Divide the chestnuts among salads and pass the pepper mill.

········

CHICKEN GIBLET STEW WITH
TINY SAUSAGE MEATBALLS AND FRESH PEAS

This recipe is from Grandma Til to the special few who love chicken giblets. She used canned peas, which were most commonly available years ago. Now fresh peas, which are most abundant in the winter, are flown in daily from everywhere, and fresh peas add a new dimension to this adaptation of her classic.

Serves 4

2½ pounds fresh chicken giblets
1 cup milk
½ pound sweet or hot Italian sausage
1 pound ripe Roma-style (plum) tomatoes
¼ cup olive oil
1 medium-size onion, peeled and cut into
 medium dice
2 stalks celery, cut into medium dice
2 carrots, peeled and cut into medium dice

5 cloves garlic, peeled and sliced fine
½ 6-ounce can tomato paste
½ teaspoon salt or to taste
½ teaspoon freshly ground black pepper
 or to taste
2 teaspoons fresh thyme leaves *or*
 1 teaspoon dried
2 pounds fresh peas, shucked

1. Wash giblets and cut into ½-inch pieces. Soak in milk for 1 hour.

2. Remove casing from sausage. Slice, then roll into small meatballs the size of cherries. Reserve on a plate. Plunge tomatoes into boiling water for a moment, then peel and squeeze out seeds. Break tomatoes into chunks.

3. In a large skillet, sauté the meatballs in one-third of the olive oil over medium heat until they are brown. Remove all but 2 tablespoons of the fat. Add the onion, celery, carrots, and garlic to skillet and sauté for about 5 minutes, until just beginning to color. Transfer vegetables to a bowl.

4. Add remaining olive oil to skillet. Drain giblets well, add to skillet, and cover, stirring frequently. Bring to a simmer and blanch giblets for 5–8 minutes. Dump giblets into a strainer, drain, and put them back in the skillet.

5. Add sausage and vegetables, tomato, tomato paste, salt, pepper, and thyme. Cover skillet and stew very slowly for 1 hour or until giblets are tender. Add peas and cook an additional 5 minutes. Stir occasionally, adding more water as necessary to keep a sauce.

· · · · · · · ·

WILD MUSHROOM POLENTA

Polenta is one of those things I could never quite accurately describe. I usually tell people about how it's made instead of trying to compare its taste to something. Originally a food for the poor, this Italian specialty is simply water and cornmeal cooked together, usually allowed to set and then sliced and reheated. When I was a boy, we would always manage to use our gas grill even under the bleakest of weather conditions, and a few slices of grilled polenta found a common place on our table. For those times when grilling just can't be done, you may prepare the polenta as directed, then reheat it by sautéing in a little butter.

Serves 4

2 ounces assorted dried wild mushrooms
1 cup hot water
2¼ cups cold water
2 teaspoons salt
1 cup stone-ground cornmeal
1 teaspoon fresh thyme leaves *or* ½
   teaspoon dried

1. Soak wild mushrooms in hot water for 10 minutes. Drain the mushrooms, reserving the liquid, and slice them into small pieces.

2. Pour mushroom liquid and cold water into a medium-size saucepan and bring to a boil. Add salt. Reduce heat until water simmers, then sprinkle in the cornmeal in a steady stream, stirring with a whisk, until all cornmeal is incorporated. Adjust heat so it bubbles every couple of seconds and cook, uncovered, for 15 minutes, stirring very often. Add the mushrooms and thyme leaves and cook for an additional 5 minutes. Pour into an oiled loaf pan and cool to room temperature. Refrigerate overnight. (Note: It's normal for the polenta to stick to the bottom of the pot; soak it in water for 20 minutes and the bottom will come clean easily.)

3. Preheat grill until very hot. Remove polenta from pan and cut into ½-inch slices. Lay them on the hot grates and grill them until marks are made, about 5 minutes. Turn and grill again. Serve warm with grilled or stewed meats.

· · · · · · · ·

GRANDMA'S BOILED CAKE
WITH HOT BUTTERED RUM SAUCE

The aroma of the boiling spices that fills the house in itself is worth preparing this dessert. Grandma Til always used some coffee instead of water in her recipe, which lends both extra flavor and color to this moist and dense cake. During the Depression it was considered an economical cake, using no eggs, and relies on baking soda to lighten the loaf. The directions must be followed precisely for the soda to work properly. Serve with the Hot Buttered Rum Sauce.

Makes 2 loaf cakes (1¼ cups sauce)

CAKE
1 1-pound box dark raisins
2 cups sugar
1 teaspoon freshly grated nutmeg
1 teaspoon salt
1 teaspoon ground cinnamon
½ teaspoon ground cloves
1¼ cups brewed black coffee
1¼ cups water
1 cup (½ pound) unsalted butter
3½ cups all-purpose flour
2 teaspoons baking soda
1 cup chopped walnuts

HOT BUTTERED RUM SAUCE
½ cup (¼ pound) unsalted butter
1 cup sugar
1 egg
¼ cup dark rum

1. Put all cake ingredients except flour, soda, and nuts in a large saucepan and bring to a boil for 2 minutes. Remove and allow to cool until comfortably warm to your fingertips.

2. Preheat oven to 350°F. Quickly stir in flour, soda, and nuts. Pour into 2 nonstick loaf pans and bake for 1 hour. Cool in pan for 15 minutes, then remove to a rack.

3. Prepare sauce by melting the butter and sugar together in the top of a double boiler. When melted, cook for an additional minute. Cool slightly. Beat the egg in a small bowl, then whisk it into the melted butter. Whisk in rum. Either serve immediately or keep warm over hot water.

· · · · · · · ·

C E L E B R A T I O N S

There is no better occasion for preparing a great meal than a holiday gathering. These celebration menus accommodate those extra-large crowds for which makeshift tables are set up, sometimes extending out of the dining room. Since kitchen space is usually a problem as well, certain dishes can be prepared by friends and brought to the party. With a little planning and forethought, these glorious celebrations can even be a celebration for the cook.

THANKSGIVING FEAST

. . . .

*Sorrel and Belgian Endive Salad with
Toasted Walnut and Roquefort Vinaigrette*

Charcoal-Grilled Hen Turkey Roasted with Garlic and Herbs

Chestnut and Sausage Stuffing

Corn Pudding

Buttered Turnip Greens

Cranberry Pear Relish

Grandma's Candied Yams

Pumpkin Custard with Brandy Cream

. . . .

This Thanksgiving Feast will stuff eight people, with ample and delicious leftovers. The meal can be quite a bit of work, but with planning you'll be able to prepare almost everything well in advance. Then gather together and enjoy this most memorable meal.

SORREL AND BELGIAN ENDIVE SALAD
WITH TOASTED WALNUT AND ROQUEFORT VINAIGRETTE

Cheeses have a season just as fruits and vegetables do, and the cold winter months are when we find the best Roquefort. Authentic Roquefort cheese comes from only one place, Roquefort, France, and it is essential for this salad. If you cannot find fresh sorrel, which has a faint lemony flavor, replace it with another pungent-tasting green, such as arugula or watercress. The Balsamic Vinaigrette only improves with age, so when you prepare it, it's wise to make a large quantity—it's quite versatile. Add the toasted walnuts and Roquefort to the salad, not the dressing.

Serves 8

2 bunches fresh sorrel leaves	1 small red onion, peeled and sliced thin
5 heads Belgian endive	1 cup Balsamic Vinaigrette (see Index)
¾ cup shelled walnuts	¼ pound Roquefort cheese

106

1. Cut sorrel into small pieces, cutting on the bias through a stack of leaves at about ¾-inch intervals. Place in cold water to wash. Cut heads of Belgian endive in a similar fashion, on the bias into ¾-inch slices. Mix together with sorrel, washing them well. Spin dry in a salad spinner or toss leaves with several paper towels. Place in refrigerator to crisp leaves.

2. Preheat oven to 350°F and toast walnuts for 8–10 minutes, until just beginning to color. Remove to a cutting board and chop coarse. Chill.

3. Just prior to serving, place the onion slices on the greens in a large bowl, pour a conservative amount of dressing over top, add half the cheese and nuts, and toss with your hands. Add more dressing as necessary. Serve on chilled plates, sprinkled with remaining walnuts and Roquefort. Pass the pepper mill.

· · · · · · · ·

CHARCOAL-GRILLED HEN TURKEY ROASTED WITH GARLIC AND HERBS

The first turkey eaten in this country was smoked over coals by the Indians. It lends itself perfectly to grilling, marinated for two days in aromatic herbs and garlic, roasted in the oven until cooked, and finished on the grill. Note that the turkey is divided into two pieces for the grilling, so if you must have a whole bird to carve at the table, you won't be able to grill. Proceed with the recipe as directed and roast until fully cooked. Hen turkeys generally weigh in at about 18 pounds and are preferred since the toms can grow quite large and can become tough and gamy. A fresh turkey is also preferred to a frozen one. Either way, it should be just barely thawed and thoroughly washed before the marinating process begins.

Serves 8 with leftovers

1 18-to-20-pound hen turkey, thawed	Leaves from 1–2 bunches fresh thyme
1 bulb garlic, peeled	(about ½ cup)
1 cup olive oil	Leaves from ½ bunch fresh rosemary
¼ cup dry sherry	(about ½ cup)
2 teaspoons freshly ground black pepper	Salt to taste

1. The morning before Thanksgiving Day, wash turkey well, inside and out. Set giblets aside. Put the peeled garlic, olive oil, sherry, pepper, and herbs in a blender and run until mixture is pureed. Place the turkey in a large doubled plastic bag. Pour some marinade into the cavity and rub it around with your fingers. Rub marinade on giblets and place them in bag as well. Pour remaining marinade over the turkey. Secure tightly with a twist tie. Roll the bird around, distributing the marinade evenly. Marinate in refrigerator for up to 2 days, at least overnight, occasionally turning the turkey over.

2. Six hours before serving, preheat oven to 325°F. Remove turkey from bag. Place on a rack in a shallow roasting pan, breast side up. Sprinkle it generously with salt, inside and out, under legs, etc. Tuck wings under and tent bird with foil. Arrange giblets around bird.

3. Roast for about 5–6 hours, depending on size, until bird is just barely done, *although fully cooked.* Very little additional cooking will occur on the grill—the cooking takes place in the oven. Test by inserting a meat thermometer into the thickest part of the thigh. It should register 170°F when the bird is cooked. There should be no traces of blood in the cavity. The juices should all be clear. When roasting is finished, remove and tent with foil in a warm place. Note: If you don't want to grill the turkey, allow the bird to rest for 20 minutes before carving. Serve with the degreased drippings.

4. To grill turkey, preheat charcoal so it will be at its hottest about 30 minutes before dinnertime. Using a large, sharp knife, carefully separate the top (breast) part of the turkey from the bottom (legs) by cutting through the base of the rib bones down toward the neck. Grill on both sides until skin is well colored and crispy. Be careful not to overcook the breast section. Remove to a work surface and cut into pieces. Remove breasts from rib cage and slice on the bias. Arrange on platter. Spoon drippings over turkey. Tent with foil until serving time.

· · · · · · · ·

CHESTNUT AND SAUSAGE STUFFING

It may be difficult to break the traditional habit of stuffing the bird, but you'll have much more cooking control if you cook the stuffing separately. This stuffing can be prepared the day before and baked at dinnertime. When you set the finished bird on a serving platter, arrange the stuffing around the outside and garnish with fresh herbs. Or serve it in its own bowl if you have many people sitting around the table. If you prefer a stuffing without sausage, try substituting one pint freshly shucked oysters.

Serves 8

1 pound fresh chestnuts
1 loaf Italian bread, cut into 1-inch cubes (about 4 cups)
1 pound sweet Italian sausage
½ cup (¼ pound) unsalted butter
1 cup diced celery with some leaves
4 cloves garlic, peeled and minced
2 large onions, peeled and chopped

1 bunch Italian (flat-leaf) parsley, chopped (about 1 cup)
¼ cup fresh sage *or* 1 tablespoon dried
3 tablespoons poultry seasoning
Salt to taste
Freshly ground pepper to taste
2 14-ounce cans chicken broth

1. Preheat oven to 425°F. Cut a small slit along the side of each chestnut with the tip of a paring knife to prevent bursting in oven. Roast for 15 minutes (do not turn oven off). Peel both shell and skin from chestnuts. Cool slightly and coarsely chop chestnuts.

2. Toast bread on a cookie sheet in hot oven until golden brown, turning once. Place in a large bowl and sprinkle with chopped chestnuts. Remove sausage from casing and sauté in a large skillet until lightly browned, about 10 minutes. Break into small pieces with a fork. Drain and sprinkle on top of the bread cubes.

3. Wipe out the skillet with a paper towel, replace on heat, and melt the butter. Add celery, garlic, and onions. Cook for about 8 minutes, until transparent. Combine with the bread mixture. Add chopped parsley, sage, and poultry seasoning. Sprinkle with salt and pepper. Add enough chicken broth to soften bread cubes without making them mushy. Toss lightly but thoroughly, adding seasonings and salt and pepper to taste.

4. Preheat oven to 350°F. Butter a 9″ × 13″ × 2″ ovenproof dish and lightly press in stuffing. Cover with foil. (Stuffing may be refrigerated for up to 24 hours at this point.) Bake, covered, for about 30 minutes. For a crisp top, remove foil during the last 15 minutes.

· · · · · · · ·

CORN PUDDING

When corn pudding is baked in a rustic-looking earthenware bowl, it just seems to taste better; certainly it looks more attractive on the table. Bake the pudding in a slow oven for at least an hour. If the oven becomes too hot, the pudding may curdle, so be careful.

Serves 8

3 cups frozen corn kernels, thawed
2 cups milk
3 eggs
1 egg yolk
¼ cup yellow cornmeal
2 teaspoons salt
2 tablespoons sugar
3 tablespoons unsalted butter

1. Preheat oven to 375°F. Butter a 1½-quart ovenproof casserole. Dry thawed corn by pressing between paper towels until all excess water has been absorbed. Combine with 1 cup of the milk in a blender; puree on high speed until smooth. Add eggs and egg yolk and blend well. Set aside.

2. Mix cornmeal, salt, sugar, and ½ cup of remaining milk in a small bowl. Scald remaining ½ cup milk with butter in a saucepan. Pour cornmeal and milk mixture gradually into the hot milk, stirring constantly. Cook over medium heat, stirring, until mixture comes to a full boil. Remove from heat.

3. Add corn puree to pot. Stir well. Pour into prepared casserole and bake in a water bath for 1 hour or until the center is firm and a knife comes out clean.

· · · · · · · ·

BUTTERED TURNIP GREENS

Perfect for a two-hour meal like Thanksgiving, because, as vegetables go, these hardy, leafy greens stay firm and fresh for quite a while after they've been cooked. If you have a microwave, reheating this dish is a perfect use for it.

Serves 8

9–10 pounds turnip greens
1 teaspoon salt or to taste
½ cup unsalted butter

1 tablespoon sugar
1 teaspoon freshly ground black pepper
  or to taste

Cut off stem part of turnip leaves and discard. Cut leaves into large pieces. Wash several times in water, drain, and pack into a large pot, using only the water that clings to the leaves to steam the greens. Cover and bring to a boil over high heat. Reduce heat, sprinkle with salt, and redistribute greens. Cover and steam for 7 minutes. Drain greens and place in a bowl. Add butter, sugar, pepper, and more salt to taste.

· · · · · · · ·

CRANBERRY PEAR RELISH

Sweet pears are a perfect contrast to tart cranberries. As the pears cook, they pick up the wonderful cranberry color that makes this relish a perfect way to enliven any grilled or roasted meal. Cranberries can be frozen raw for many months without losing their character. Once made, the relish keeps for over a week in the refrigerator.

Serves 8

4 firm, ripe pears, such as d'Anjou or
   Bartlett
2 cups water
2 cups sugar
2 12-ounce bags fresh cranberries
2 cinnamon sticks

1. Peel pears and, without coring them, cut into ½-inch squares; remove seeds. Bring water and sugar to a boil. Add pears, cranberries, and cinnamon sticks.

2. Return to a boil and simmer for 12 minutes, stirring frequently. Cool to room temperature in the pan; then transfer relish to a clear glass serving bowl. Refrigerate until serving time.

· · · · · · · ·

GRANDMA'S CANDIED YAMS

It's a shame that so many great recipes are known only to their creators. For example, my grandmother Til was responsible for the candied yams at every appropriate celebration. This is my best attempt to re-create her magic.

Serves 8

4-5 pounds yams
1 cup dark brown sugar
1 cup water
¼ cup unsalted butter
1 clove

1. Place yams in a large pot and cover with hot water. Lightly salt the water and bring to a boil. Allow the yams to simmer until almost cooked. Check doneness with a skewer—they should be cooked but still firm in the center.

2. Meanwhile, combine remaining ingredients in a small saucepan and bring to a simmer. Continue to simmer until liquid has reduced to a light syrup about the consistency of pancake syrup. Stir occasionally.

3. When yams are done, drain them and peel them while they are hot. Allow to cool. Cut large yams into lengthwise quarters and smaller ones in half. Arrange in a glass casserole in a single layer. Drizzle syrup over yams.

4. You may now bake them immediately or keep them at room temperature for several hours, then bake. It is important to baste them often with the syrup in which they are cooking. The oven temperature is not that important, somewhere between 350° and 425°F, depending on how quickly you want them to be finished. They are ready when they are hot and bubbly. The syrup should be reduced to a glaze and spooned over the yams.

· · · · · · · ·

PUMPKIN CUSTARD WITH BRANDY CREAM

Dessert after a Thanksgiving feast can be superfluous, but this custard is light and delicate, perfectly completing the meal.

Serves 8

4 eggs
3 egg yolks
¼ teaspoon salt
1 cup plus 2 tablespoons sugar
½ teaspoon ground cinnamon
¼ teaspoon freshly grated nutmeg
Pinch of ground cloves
Pinch of ground allspice
Pinch of ground ginger
3 cups milk
1 cup half-and-half
1 teaspoon vanilla extract
1⅓ cups canned pumpkin
1 cup whipping cream
1 tablespoon brandy

1. Combine eggs, egg yolks, salt, 1 cup sugar, and spices in the top of a double boiler over simmering water. Blend with wooden spoon. Add milk and half-and-half. Cook until mixture thickens enough to coat the spoon. Water should never boil. Strain immediately into a large bowl, add vanilla, and fold in pumpkin. Divide among eight individual cups and chill thoroughly.

2. No more than an hour before serving, whip cream with remaining 2 tablespoons sugar. Whip in brandy. Top each dessert with a spoonful of brandy cream.

· · · · · · · ·

AN ITALIAN CHRISTMAS EVE

· · · · · · · ·

Southern Italian Focaccia with
Sautéed Escarole, Black Olives, and Capers

Marinated Salt Cod in Garlic and Extra-Virgin Oil
on Curly Endive Greens

Crisp Fried Baby Calamari and Smelts
with Charred Red Pepper Cream

Penne Tossed with Broccoli, Garlic, and Extra-Virgin Oil

Handmade Parsley Linguine and Fresh Clam Sauce

Angelo's Zuppa di Pesce

Shredded Brussels Sprout Sauté

Honey Struffoli

Rum Eggnog Punch

Grandma's Coconut Fruitcake

· · · · · · · ·

Christmas Eve to Italians, and to other nationalities as well, is traditionally a day when no meat is eaten. The preparation for the feast begins early in the week as fruitcakes are baked and pastas are made. In my family there were always many helpers, and everyone was given specific responsibilities. All the food was placed on the table at the onset of the meal, and everyone ate a little of everything. This menu will serve about 12 people. If you are fewer, make just one entrée and a dessert, with some focaccia and a salad.

SOUTHERN ITALIAN FOCACCIA WITH
SAUTEED ESCAROLE, BLACK OLIVES, AND CAPERS
········

This is a traditional Christmas dish in the Campania region of Italy. Though Italians make focaccia all through the year, this unique topping is usually saved for the holidays. The topping for the basic focaccia can be replaced by a similar sauté of many vegetables, such as mushrooms, shredded artichokes, sun-dried tomatoes, or (my favorite) simply sliced raw onion, minced garlic, drizzled extra-virgin olive oil, and a sprinkle of salt, pepper, and chopped fresh rosemary. The yield of this recipe depends on how you cut the focaccia and how large a baking pan you have. You may also prefer to bake two smaller versions. The thickness of the dough isn't all that important; about ¾ inch is best.

Serves 12

FOCACCIA
1 cup almost-lukewarm water
1 18-gram cake fresh yeast
1 small onion, peeled and chopped
  coarse
3 cloves garlic, peeled
1 tablespoon finely chopped fresh
  rosemary
1½ tablespoons extra-virgin olive oil
2 teaspoons salt
3½ cups unbleached bread flour
Vegetable shortening for greasing

TOPPING
2 tablespoons olive oil
3 cloves garlic, peeled and minced
2 canned anchovy fillets, rinsed with
  water
2 heads escarole, washed, drained, and
  chopped
¼ cup sliced pitted black Italian olives
2 tablespoons drained capers
1 tablespoon pine nuts
2 tablespoons white raisins, plumped in
  water or wine
Salt to taste
Freshly ground black pepper to taste

1. To prepare focaccia, combine ½ cup of the water and all the yeast in a large mixer bowl. Let rest for 10 minutes. Meanwhile, puree together the onion, garlic, rosemary, and remaining water in a blender. Add to yeast along with olive oil and salt. Begin to knead with the dough hook attachment of your mixer (or by hand), adding 1 cup flour, incorporating, then adding another. Continue with the flour, adding just enough to form a smooth, elastic ball that doesn't stick to the bowl. After about 5 minutes, remove from machine, oil the bowl and top of dough, and allow to rise in a warm, draft-free place until doubled, about 1½ hours.

2. Meanwhile, prepare topping by heating olive oil in a large skillet over medium heat. Add garlic and anchovies, mashing them well with a fork, and cook for several minutes. Add escarole and mix. Turn up heat and cook, uncovered, until escarole wilts. Drain liquid and stir in olives, capers, pine nuts, and raisins. Season with salt and black pepper. Allow to cool.

3. Generously grease the bottom of a baking sheet at least 12″ × 18″ or larger, depending on the size of your oven. Turn out dough and stretch to fit pan, allowing it to relax for several minutes before stretching again. Arrange topping over focaccia and allow to rise a second time, until the thickness of the dough has almost doubled, about 1 hour.

4. Preheat oven to 425°F. Drizzle the top of the focaccia with a bit of extra-virgin olive oil and press your fingertips oven the entire surface, making even, well-spaced indentations. Bake for about 45 minutes or until bottom of focaccia is golden brown when lifted. Cool slightly before cutting into 2″ × 4″ bars.

· · · · · · · ·

MARINATED SALT COD IN GARLIC AND EXTRA-VIRGIN OIL ON CURLY ENDIVE GREENS

Italians begin eating what they call *baccalà* as children, and not for any good reason but that it's part of their cuisine and tastes superb. This specially salted cod fillet is usually found in Italian shops and comes skinned, boned, and in large wooden crates shipped from Italy. You must rejuvenate the fish before it's cooked by soaking in lots of changes of cold water. Grandma used to leave the water drizzling into the sink all night long to wash away the salt. It's probably more convenient for you to soak it in a large bowl and change the water about six times over a 24-hour period. It can be prepared many ways, but my favorite is still the simplest. You can garnish this salad with a few roasted red pepper strips if you'd like and serve with a warm crusty bread.

Serves 12 as an appetizer

3 medium-size salt cod fillets, about 4½
    pounds
¾ cup extra-virgin olive oil
12 cloves garlic, peeled and sliced
    lengthwise as thin as possible
Juice of 2 lemons
¼ cup chopped Italian (flat-leaf) parsley
    leaves
Freshly ground black pepper to taste
3 heads curly endive
½ cup Balsamic Vinaigrette (see Index) or
    oil and vinegar
Roasted red bell pepper strips (optional)
    for garnish (see Index)

116

1. Soak the cod for 24 hours, changing the water several times. Drain cod, cut into pieces, and boil for 20 minutes. Meanwhile, heat olive oil in a small saucepan over low heat; add garlic and cook until soft but not browned, about 10 minutes.

2. When fish is done, drain and remove any skin and bones. Flake the fish into a bowl. Squeeze in lemon juice and toss lightly. Add parsley to warm olive oil, swirl pan around, and pour over fish. Toss, adding black pepper to taste. This is best if made ahead of time and allowed to marinate several hours or overnight.

3. Trim the tough ends off the endive leaves and tear the lettuce into small pieces. Toss lightly with a vinaigrette or just oil and vinegar. Arrange on individual plates or one large platter. Arrange cod over top and garnish with strips of roasted red pepper. Marinated cod keeps well in the refrigerator.

. . . .

CRISP FRIED BABY CALAMARI AND SMELTS
WITH CHARRED RED PEPPER CREAM

In southern Italy and Sicily, where squid and smelt are a part of everyone's life, they are usually eaten with only a squeeze of fresh lemon. I prefer to dip these seafoods into something spicy, such as this addictive pepper cream.

Serves 6 as a main course, 12 as a side dish

CHARRED RED PEPPER CREAM
1 large red bell pepper
1 cup sour cream
½ cup mayonnaise
¼ cup chopped Italian (flat-leaf) parsley
   leaves
½ teaspoon salt or to taste
½ teaspoon cayenne pepper or to taste
½ teaspoon sugar
2 cloves garlic, peeled
Freshly ground pepper to taste

FISH
3 pounds baby squid, cleaned
2 pounds small smelt, cleaned
2 cups all-purpose flour
1 cup white or yellow cornmeal
1 tablespoon salt
1 teaspoon freshly ground black pepper
1 teaspoon cayenne pepper
Vegetable oil for frying
Lemon wedges for garnish

1. Prepare cream by roasting pepper over a gas flame or under a preheated broiler until skin is black and blistered. Put in a plastic bag for 5 minutes to steam. Peel off black skin, rinsing your fingertips, not the pepper, in running water; discard seeds. Place pepper in a food processor or blender. Add remaining ingredients and puree until smooth. Season with salt and pepper as necessary. Pour into serving dish and refrigerate. May be made the day before.

2. To clean squid further, remove everything from inside the white squid bodies and slice them into ¼-inch rings. Squeeze out the beak (a small white ball) from the base of the tentacles; discard. Cut large tentacles in half. Wash all squid and smelt with cold water. Drain well.

3. Combine flour, cornmeal, salt, and peppers in a large plastic bag. Add the wet fish and toss them in the bag, assuring that they are evenly floured. Remove to a colander and flip to sift off flour.

4. Heat ¾ inch oil in a large skillet over high heat. Reduce heat slightly and add some of the squid and smelt but don't crowd the pan. Fry quickly until golden brown and remove to paper towels. Continue with remaining fish, adding oil as necessary. If the oil is not hot enough, the fish won't get crispy. When finished, arrange on a serving platter, sprinkle with salt to taste, and garnish with lemon wedges. Serve hot with the roasted red pepper cream.

. . . .

PENNE TOSSED WITH BROCCOLI, GARLIC, AND EXTRA-VIRGIN OIL

This is a combination of four or five basic Italian flavorings. The key is the balance of ingredients. It is very important to cook this dish to the correct degree of doneness. The broccoli must be soft enough to break apart slightly but not turn to mush. You may also refrigerate the finished pasta for an easy pasta salad.

Serves 6 as a main course, 12 as a side dish

2 large bunches broccoli
¾ cup extra-virgin olive oil
6–8 cloves garlic, peeled and sliced fine
½ teaspoon hot red pepper flakes (optional)
Approximately 1 teaspoon salt or to taste
Approximately 1 teaspoon freshly ground black pepper or to taste
2 teaspoons sugar
¼ cup fresh basil leaves, julienned
1½ pounds dried penne
4 tablespoons unsalted butter
½ cup grated Parmesan cheese or to taste

1. Put salted water on to boil. Trim broccoli to flowerets and wash in colander. Heat 4 tablespoons of the olive oil in a large skillet. Add garlic and red pepper flakes. Slowly sauté until beginning to color; add broccoli, salt, pepper, and sugar. Sauté broccoli for a minute or 2 over medium-high heat. Add basil and a small cup of water, cover, and cook broccoli until very tender, adding more water as necessary. When you're done, the broccoli should be quite soft and almost falling apart.

2. Boil pasta as directed in "Dried Pasta" (see Index) and add to broccoli. Add butter and stir with remaining extra-virgin olive oil, salt and pepper to taste, and Parmesan cheese, mixing well. Serve with a crusty bread at the table.

· · · · · · · ·

HANDMADE PARSLEY LINGUINE AND FRESH CLAM SAUCE

The homemade parsley linguine can be prepared in advance of your celebration. It can be wrapped in plastic and refrigerated for up to three days. Fresh clams come in all sizes, and you'll find the best for this pasta are littlenecks, which have a shell diameter of less than two inches. It's very important that the clams be alive when cooked. Live clams keep their shells tightly closed; if they are open and don't respond when squeezed, discard them. Store clams in the refrigerator in an open container for up to two days. To ensure tender clams, cook them just until they open.

Serves 6 as a main course, 12 as a side dish

PARSLEY LINGUINE
⅓ cup roughly chopped Italian (flat-leaf)
   parsley leaves
4 cups all-purpose flour
6 eggs
1 teaspoon salt
1 tablespoon extra-virgin olive oil

FRESH CLAM SAUCE
½ cup extra-virgin olive oil
6 cloves garlic, peeled and minced
½ teaspoon hot red pepper flakes
4 pounds small fresh clams, scrubbed
   well
1 cup dry white wine
2 pounds Roma-style (plum) tomatoes,
   peeled and seeded (see Index)
¾ cup chopped Italian (flat-leaf) parsley
   leaves
6 basil leaves, shredded fine
2 teaspoons salt or to taste
½ teaspoon freshly ground black pepper
   or to taste

1. Prepare the linguine in the food processor (see "Food Processor Pasta" in Index), adding parsley leaves at the beginning along with flour, eggs, and remaining ingredients. Cut into linguine as directed (see "Rolling Dough with a Pasta Machine" in Index) and store in refrigerator on a kitchen towel. Keep covered with plastic wrap.

2. To prepare the sauce, heat olive oil in a large pot. Add garlic, red pepper flakes, and clams. Cook over medium-high heat for 1 minute, tossing well. Add wine, cover, and steam just until clams open. Remove clams from pot, leaving liquid in pan. Add tomatoes, parsley, basil, salt, and pepper. Simmer for 5 minutes.

3. Meanwhile, remove clams from shells. When sauce is complete, add clams and turn off heat.

4. Boil pasta in salted water for a minute or 2, until al dente, and toss with clam sauce.

. . . .

120

ANGELO'S ZUPPA DI PESCE

Zuppa di pesce means "fish soup," and the choice of fish is up to the individual chef. My dear friend Angelo offered this exceptional delicacy at his renowned restaurant on the Italian Riviera named Locanda dell'Angelo only on special nights and then only for his best customers. The fish must be fresh, not frozen, no matter what the fishmonger tells you. Stick with whatever is fresh that day and never compromise. Be alert for labels that say "fresh frozen" fish. All this means is that they thawed it out for you.

Serves 6 as a main course, 12 as a side dish

2 pounds sea bass, cod, or other firm white fish, all bones removed
Salt to taste
Freshly ground black pepper to taste
All-purpose flour for dusting
1 pound baby squid, cleaned
1 1-pound loaf Italian bread, cut into ½-inch slices
3 cloves garlic, peeled
⅓ cup extra-virgin olive oil, plus additional oil for croutons
3 cloves garlic, peeled and minced
¼ cup chopped celery leaves
¼ cup chopped Italian (flat-leaf) parsley

1 pound Roma-style (plum) tomatoes, peeled and seeded (see Index)
½ cup dry white wine
¼ cup dry vermouth
2 tablespoons dry sherry
3 tablespoons unsalted butter
1 10-ounce bottle clam juice
2–3 dashes of Tabasco sauce, to taste
½ teaspoon Worcestershire sauce
1 pound jumbo shrimp, peeled and deveined
8 mussels
16 littleneck or other small clams
1 lemon, cut into 8 wedges

1. Slice the fish into 2-inch pieces. Sprinkle with salt and pepper and dust with flour. Clean and cut squid as described in Crisp Fried Baby Calamari (see Index). Toast bread under preheated broiler. Rub both sides of each slice with whole garlic cloves. Drizzle lightly with additional olive oil. Arrange on the bottom of a large, deep serving platter.

2. In a very large sauté pan, heat ⅓ cup olive oil over medium-high heat. Add minced garlic, celery leaves, and parsley, sauté for a moment, then add tomatoes, white wine, vermouth, sherry, and 1 tablespoon of the butter. Add clam juice, Tabasco, and Worcestershire and mix well. Adjust heat to a simmer. Lay in floured fish fillets. On top of fillets, place the shrimp. Arrange mussels, clams, and lemon wedges around fillets, cover, and simmer until clams open and fish is no longer opaque, about 5 minutes. Arrange all fish over croutons with a slotted spoon; if the clams aren't open but the fish is cooked, remove fish to serving platter and continue to cook clams as necessary.

3. Bring juices to a simmer again and add squid. As soon as liquid returns to a simmer, add remaining butter and continue to stir until it's incorporated. Taste and

adjust salt and pepper if needed. Squid cooks quickly, in about 2 minutes, just until tender. Pour broth and squid over fish and serve hot.

· · · · · · · ·

SHREDDED BRUSSELS SPROUT SAUTE

This is the only way I have ever truly enjoyed brussels sprouts. I guess it's because of how the sprouts are sliced; those whole round heads bothered me as a child, and I never forgot it. The recipe can also be prepared and stirred into cooked pasta or rice, making an appetizing one-course dinner.

Serves 12 as a side dish

4 pounds brussels sprouts
¼ cup extra-virgin olive oil
6 cloves garlic, peeled and minced
½ cup fresh basil leaves, gathered and
   shredded fine
1 teaspoon sugar
1 teaspoon salt or to taste
¼ teaspoon hot red pepper flakes or to
   taste
Freshly ground black pepper to taste
½ cup chicken broth, vegetable broth, or
   water
2 tablespoons grated Parmesan cheese

1. Peel outer leaves off brussels sprouts; trim bottoms. Wash them, then cut them in half through the root. Lay each half flat on a cutting board and slice as thin as you can, through the root. Reserve in a bowl.

2. Heat olive oil in a large skillet over medium-high heat. Add garlic, basil, and brussels sprouts and sauté for 2 minutes. Sprinkle with sugar and seasonings and add broth. Cook quickly over high heat, uncovered, tossing often until brussels sprouts are tender, about 6 minutes. Add additional broth or water as necessary just to prevent scorching. Add Parmesan and taste for salt and pepper.

· · · · · · · ·

122

HONEY STRUFFOLI

A struffoli is made up of pea-sized puffs of dough that are fried quickly, tossed with honey and pine nuts, then formed into a mound and allowed to set. It's an important tradition for an Italian Christmas celebration, though no one really knows why. In my family it was always used as a centerpiece on the table when family and guests arrived. Serve the sticky, clustered dough by breaking off individual pieces onto plates; it always tastes better when you pick at it with your fingertips.

Serve 10–12

Vegetable oil for frying
2 cups all-purpose flour, sifted
¼ teaspoon salt
3 eggs
½ teaspoon vanilla extract
1 cup honey
1 tablespoon sugar
¼ cup pine nuts, lightly toasted
1 tablespoon tiny multicolored sprinkles
　for garnish (optional)

1. Heat 1 inch of oil in a deep saucepan over medium heat and keep it at about 365°F.

2. Place flour and salt in a large bowl. Make a well in the center of flour. Add eggs, one at a time, mixing slightly after each. Add vanilla and mix well to form a soft dough. Turn dough out onto a lightly floured surface and knead for 1 minute. Divide dough in half. Lightly roll out each half ¼ inch thick to form a rectangle. Cut dough with a pastry cutter into strips ¼ inch wide. Use palm of hand to roll strips to pencil thickness. Cut into pea-sized pieces about ¼–½ inch long.

3. Fry as many pieces of dough as will float uncrowded, one layer deep, in fat. Fry for 3–5 minutes, stirring occasionally during frying. Remove with slotted spoon and drain on paper towels. Meanwhile, cook honey and sugar in a small pot over medium heat for 5 minutes. Add pine nuts. Remove from heat, combine with deep-fried dough, and stir well until coated with honey. Chill for a moment in the refrigerator, then remove to a large serving platter, shaping the pieces into a large mound. Sprinkle with candies to garnish if desired. Chill in refrigerator.

. . . .

RUM EGGNOG PUNCH

A holiday is not complete without a good rum punch. The key here is separating the eggs for whipping—it makes the punch light and frothy. You can vary the amount of rum you use, but remember, since it's so rich only a small glass is served, so just a small amount should pack a hefty punch of its own.

Serves 12–14 (2½ quarts)

1 quart cold heavy cream
1 cup cold milk
1 cup Jamaican dark rum
1 teaspoon vanilla extract
6 eggs, separated, at room temperature
1 cup sugar
freshly grated nutmeg

1. Mix the cream, milk, rum, and vanilla in a large bowl or pitcher. Beat the egg yolks and half the sugar in a stainless-steel bowl until pale and light. Gradually whisk egg mixture into cream mixture. Chill for 2 hours.

2. In another bowl, whip egg whites, gradually adding remaining sugar, until soft peaks form, stiff but not dry. Fold them gently into the cream mixture. Sprinkle top with nutmeg.

· · · · · · · ·

GRANDMA'S COCONUT FRUITCAKE

Fruitcakes do *not* have to be inedible, as proven by my grandmother Til's recipe. She never used any candied citron, which normally abounds in fruitcakes, and maybe that's why I love this so much. It's very special, and the sweet taste of the coconut raises it several levels above the ordinary. When I was a child, every Christmas package ever received from my grandmother contained several of these special cakes wrapped in red foil and strung with ribbon.

Makes 6 4" × 8" fruitcakes

1 fresh coconut
½ pound candied red cherries
½ pound candied green cherries
1 pound candied pineapple (not citron)
1 pound golden raisins
½ pound (2 cups) shelled walnuts
½ pound (2 cups) shelled pecans
2 cups (1 pound) salted butter, softened

1 pound (2 cups) sugar
4 cups all-purpose flour
1 teaspoon cream of tartar
1 teaspoon baking soda
6 eggs
4 teaspoons vanilla extract
½ fifth cognac or brandy

1. Open coconut by carefully pounding a screwdriver through its "eye" with a hammer. Empty the coconut milk into a very large bowl. Crack open the fruit, using a hammer as necessary. Peel off shell and grate all coconut with a grater. Put into bowl with coconut milk.

2. Add candied cherries, candied pineapple, and raisins to coconut. Coarsely chop nuts with a large knife. Add to fruit. Set aside. Lightly grease (or spray with vegetable spray) six 4" × 8" aluminum loaf pans. Preheat oven to 300°F.

3. Cream butter and sugar together. Mix flour, cream of tartar, and baking soda together in another bowl. Add eggs, one by one, to butter, mixing well after each addition. Add vanilla. Add flour mixture in three parts, mixing just until all flour is incorporated. Stir in fruit mixture and mix well by hand with a large spatula, making sure you scrape the bottom of the bowl. Divide fruitcake mix among prepared loaf pans, pressing it in with the tip of the spatula. Space evenly in oven and bake for 1¼–1½ hours or until golden and toothpick inserted in the center comes out clean. Do not overbake.

4. Allow to cool for 10 minutes. Paint generously with brandy while still in pans. Cool for 30 minutes longer, remove from pans, then wrap tightly in plastic wrap. Refrigerate for 5 days. Fruitcakes may then be frozen or kept in the refrigerator for up to 1 month. Bring to room temperature before serving.

· · · · · · · ·

FESTIVE CELEBRATION

· · · · · · · ·

Fennel and Garlic Soup with Parmesan Bruschette

Tossed Caesar Salad with Shaved Parmesan Cheese

Scallop and Shrimp Ravioli in Calamari Butter Sauce

Tangerine Ice

Herb-Roasted Holiday Capon

Steamed Persimmon Pudding with Brandy Sauce

· · · · · · · ·

This festive celebration is for people who like to entertain during the holidays. Almost everything on this menu can be made before guests arrive. The menu is best when served course by course, which means, unless you have a butler, you'll probably want to recruit a helper. You may want to add a seasonal vegetable to accompany the capon, selecting a recipe that can be made ahead of time and perhaps reheated in the microwave, such as peas or broccoli. You may also want to serve some Cranberry Pear Relish (see Index) or other colorful relishes to accompany the roasted capon. Your favorite dry white wine or champagne may be served throughout this celebration, ending with freshly brewed coffee and Steamed Persimmon Pudding. This festive celebration serves eight people. If you're cooking for fewer guests, eliminate either the ravioli or the capon and serve only one, along with the soup, salad, and, of course, dessert.

FENNEL AND GARLIC SOUP WITH PARMESAN BRUSCHETTE

Garlic gives this soup a special sweetness, and the scent of fresh fennel makes it a unique and satisfying complement to any winter or holiday menu. As with most soups, you can make this well in advance and reheat to serve. This recipe is enough for six to eight people; if you're cooking for more, it doubles easily.

Serves 8 (8 cups)

2 large bulbs fennel
½ cup (¼ pound) unsalted butter
1 bulb garlic cloves, peeled and halved
2 medium-size onions, peeled and
  chopped
¼ cup all-purpose flour
2 quarts hot chicken broth
Salt to taste
Freshly ground black pepper to taste
16 slices day-old French bread baguette,
  approximately ¼ inch thick
Approximately 5 cloves garlic, peeled
⅓ cup extra-virgin olive oil
¼ cup grated Parmesan cheese

1. Trim feathery tops off fennel, chop fine, and reserve. Coarsely chop fennel bulb. In a large soup pot, melt the butter over medium-low heat. Add the garlic, onion, and chopped fennel bulb and sweat for 5 minutes without browning. Add ¼ cup flour, cook for 2 minutes longer, stirring, and remove from heat. Pour in hot chicken broth and return pot to heat; bring to a boil, cover, and simmer over low heat until garlic and fennel are completely soft, about 25–30 minutes. Remove from heat.

2. Strain the vegetables and a small amount of broth into a blender or food processor. Puree and return to pot with remaining broth. Add salt and pepper to taste and reheat gently. Stir in chopped fennel tops. (Soup may be made the day before and reheated to serve.)

3. To prepare bruschette, preheat broiler. Place bread slices on baking sheet and toast on one side under the broiler until golden. Rub the toasted sides with the peeled garlic cloves. Turn bruschette over and sprinkle each generously with olive oil. Sprinkle a pinch of Parmesan over each and broil until light brown and crispy. Serve while still warm to accompany soup.

· · · · · · · ·

TOSSED CAESAR SALAD WITH SHAVED PARMESAN CHEESE

The perfect Caesar salad is the one that tastes great to you. It's important to be flexible with the quantities of ingredients you use—feel free to add or decrease any of the flavorings but not the oil or eggs. If you prefer extra garlic or anchovy or less lemon, make the changes, taste, and correct the seasonings.

Serves 8

DRESSING
3 egg yolks
Juice of 1 lemon
3 cloves garlic
1 teaspoon freshly ground black pepper
4 dashes of Tabasco sauce
4–6 anchovy fillets, rinsed
2 tablespoons Dijon mustard
2 teaspoons salt
1 teaspoon dried oregano
½ teaspoon Worcestershire sauce
¼ cup rice wine vinegar or red wine vinegar
1 cup olive oil
1 cup vegetable oil

SALAD
2 heads romaine lettuce
½ cup grated Parmesan cheese
Parmesan cheese for shaving
Anchovy fillets for garnish (optional)

1. Combine all dressing ingredients except vinegar and oils in a blender until smooth. Remove center cap from blender lid so you can pour in oils. Turn blender on and slowly add oil to whirling egg yolk mixture in a fine, steady stream until an emulsification occurs, similar to mayonnaise. After 1 cup of oil, add the vinegar. Continue with remaining oil. If dressing becomes too stiff, add a small amount of water, just enough to keep it swirling. The final result should resemble a thin mayonnaise. Correct seasoning with salt. It should be quite powerful. Refrigerate until use. Extra dressing can be used for another salad within a few days.

2. Prepare lettuce by removing outer leaves of romaine. Make two cuts lengthwise through the head, then cut crosswise into 2-inch pieces. Wash well, spin dry in salad spinner (or toss with paper towels), and refrigerate until chilled and crisp.

3. In a large bowl, toss lettuce with grated Parmesan and several heaped tablespoons of the dressing. Toss well, adding more dressing as desired. The dressing should be distributed evenly through the salad. Serve on chilled plates. Shave the side of a block of Parmesan cheese carefully with a sharp knife. Arrange shavings on salad. Garnish with anchovy fillets if desired. Pass the pepper mill.

· · · · · · · ·

SCALLOP AND SHRIMP RAVIOLI IN CALAMARI BUTTER SAUCE

These are my favorite ravioli. I learned to make them from my friend Angelo, whose phenomenal restaurant in Liguria, Italy, named Locanda dell'Angelo, served them as a specialty of the house. The kitchen staff would make the ravioli to order, boil them, and toss them with the sauce. Individual orders were made in individual skillets and served immediately—normal procedure in a restaurant kitchen. At home, since we unfortunately don't have a line of cooks and dishwashers, I have adapted Angelo's creation, as well as I could, to keep your brow dry at dinnertime. You can make these ravioli a week ahead of time and, if you'd like, freeze them.

Serves 8 (about 32 ravioli)

RAVIOLI
10 ounces scallops, any size
1 pound cod, sea bass, or other white fish
  fillets
¼ cup extra-virgin olive oil
10 ounces shrimp, any size, peeled and
  deveined
¼ cup chopped Italian (flat-leaf) parsley
1 cup fresh white bread crumbs
3 tablespoons heavy cream
3 eggs
2 egg yolks
Salt to taste
Freshly ground pepper to taste
Fresh pasta for 4 (see Index)
2 tablespoons water

CALAMARI BUTTER SAUCE
3 tablespoons olive oil
3 cloves garlic, peeled and minced
3 tablespoons chopped Italian (flat-leaf)
  parsley
½ pound baby squid pieces, well cleaned
¼ pound scallops, large ones cut in half
¼ pound tiny shrimp, peeled and
  deveined
¼ pound fresh crabmeat, flaked
¼ cup dry vermouth
10 ounces bottled clam juice
¼ cup peeled, seeded, and chopped fresh
  tomato (see "Tomatoes" in Index)
½ teaspoon Worcestershire sauce
Tabasco sauce to taste
3 tablespoons unsalted butter at room
  temperature
Salt to taste
Freshly ground pepper to taste

1. To prepare the filling, remove the small white membrane from the side of any scallop that still has one. Cut out all bones from fish fillets and cut them into 2″ × 2″ pieces. Heat olive oil in a large skillet over medium-high heat. Add shrimp, fish, scallops, and parsley. Cook quickly just until fish becomes opaque. Remove from heat and allow to cool slightly. Remove seafood with a slotted spoon to a cutting board and dice it small, nothing larger than ½ inch. Set aside. Reserve juices.

2. Place bread crumbs in a large bowl and moisten with cream. Spoon fish mixture over crumbs and add 2 eggs and the egg yolks. Mix. Add fish juices as necessary to achieve a moist, not wet, stuffing. Season generously with salt and pepper. Refrigerate.

3. Prepare the fresh pasta as directed in "Handmade Pasta Dough" (see Index). Beat remaining egg with water and a pinch of salt. After pasta rests for 1 hour, cut one slice from the dough and roll it out using a pasta machine, keeping it as wide as you can. Cover remaining dough while you work. Flour the work surface and cut the strip into 2-inch squares. Paint one square lightly with egg wash, place a heaped tablespoon of filling in center, cover with another square of pasta, and seal, pressing out air. Cut out with a round, scalloped cookie cutter or an inverted glass. Boil them immediately or place them on a kitchen towel and allow to air-dry for several hours, until pasta is dry. Flip them after an hour. Freeze on a cookie sheet, then store in a sealed container in the freezer until boiling time. Do not thaw.

4. Prepare sauce by heating the olive oil in a large skillet over medium-high heat. Toss in garlic and cook for 30 seconds. Add parsley and all seafood. Sauté quickly for 2 minutes. Add vermouth, clam juice, tomato, Worcestershire, and a few drops of Tabasco. Remove from heat and whisk in butter. Add salt and pepper to taste. May be made ahead of time and reheated when the ravioli are added.

5. To cook ravioli, bring a large pot of salted water to a boil. Drop ravioli into boiling water and cook until pasta is done, about 5 minutes, longer if frozen. Remove with a slotted spoon directly to the hot sauce. Allow to rest in the sauce over low heat for several minutes before serving.

· · · · · · · ·

TANGERINE ICE

The perfect midpoint to your celebration, this ice is made from freshly squeezed winter tangerine juice. For convenience you should prepare this ice the day before and freeze. When your guests arrive, move the frozen ice to the refrigerator so it can soften a bit before serving time.

Makes 1 quart, serving 8

1 quart freshly squeezed tangerine juice
1¼ cups sugar
juice of 1 lemon

1. In a saucepan, heat half the tangerine juice with the sugar just until it dissolves. Add remaining tangerine juice along with lemon juice. Cool to room temperature. Pour into a shallow pan and set in the freezer. As the ice begins to freeze, stir the

mixture with a wire whip and return to freezer. Repeat until it forms a thick slush, then allow it to freeze solid.

2. To serve, set in refrigerator for about 30 minutes so it softens enough to be scooped. Garnish with a sprig of mint or a tangerine leaf.

. . . .

HERB-ROASTED HOLIDAY CAPON

A capon is a special roasting chicken that's gelded when young and allowed to grow larger than regular chickens. This procedure makes the bird grow fat, and the meat is moist with an exceptional flavor. Cooking a capon slowly melts the fat and bastes the meat naturally. Capons weigh in at six to nine pounds, and you should purchase about one pound per person. Fresh organic birds are always worth searching for, but if all you can find is frozen, thaw it for a day in the refrigerator. When cooking for a crowd, you may prefer to roast the bird well in advance, then carve it and arrange it in a serving casserole. Cover it with foil and reheat in the oven before serving.

Serves 8

1 fresh capon, about 9 pounds	3 tablespoons fresh sage *or* 1½
1 small onion, peeled	tablespoons dried
8 cloves garlic, peeled	¼ cup fresh rosemary leaves
½ cup olive oil	3 tablespoons fresh thyme leaves
1 teaspoon freshly ground black pepper	1½ teaspoons salt

1. Thoroughly wash the capon inside and out with cold water. Prepare the marinade by combining the onion, garlic, olive oil, pepper, and herbs in a food processor until pureed. Place a rack in a large roasting pan. Pick up bird and sprinkle generously with salt. Rub inside and out with marinade. Place on the rack, breast up. Tuck the wings and enclose legs under flap of skin.

2. To roast, preheat oven to 325°F. Roast capon for about 25 minutes per pound, about 4 hours for a 9-pound bird. Roast until tender and juices from cavity run clear. Remove from oven and allow to rest for 15 minutes, tented with foil.

3. Remove bird to a carving surface. Remove bottom quarters, separate leg from thigh, remove breasts and cut them into pieces, and remove wings. Remove all other meat you can and arrange in a serving casserole. Siphon off the drippings with a bulb baster (leaving the fat in the pan) and drizzle over capon. Cover with foil until serving.

. . . .

STEAMED PERSIMMON PUDDING WITH BRANDY SAUCE

Persimmons have a nectarlike quality that keeps this festive pudding moist and sweet. The persimmon is an overlooked fruit that comes around only for the holidays each year. The trees grow in abundance all over Europe and take an exceptionally long time to ripen their bright orange fruit, which hangs on the limbs well after the leaves have fallen for the winter. This pudding is steamed in a special pudding mold. Once cooked, cooled, and wrapped in plastic, it freezes very well; to reheat, resteam for several minutes or warm in the microwave. It's a rich dessert, so serve small slices.

Serves about 12 (1¼ cups sauce)

PERSIMMON PUDDING
2 tablespoons unsalted butter, softened,
   plus butter to grease pudding mold
2 tablespoons sugar for pudding mold
½ cup packed dark raisins
½ cup packed golden raisins
½ cup brandy
Approximately 2 persimmons, peeled and
   pureed in food processor or blender
   (1¼ cups)
1¼ cups sugar
1 cup plus 2 tablespoons all-purpose
   flour
1 teaspoon baking soda
½ teaspoon salt
1 teaspoon ground cinnamon
½ teaspoon ground cardamom
¼ teaspoon ground cloves
¼ teaspoon freshly grated nutmeg
1 cup (about ¼ pound) shelled pecans,
   toasted and chopped coarse
½ cup half-and-half
2 egg whites

BRANDY SAUCE
½ cup (¼ pound) unsalted butter
1 cup sugar
1 egg
¼ cup brandy

132

1. To prepare pudding, butter the lid and sides of a 2-quart pudding mold (use about 2 tablespoons). Dust with about 2 tablespoons sugar. Prepare a heavy, deep pot for steaming by placing a trivet or small rack on the bottom of pot. Place the unfilled mold on the rack and pour in enough cold water to come halfway to two-thirds up the mold. Remove mold and bring water to a simmer while preparing pudding.

2. Combine raisins and plump in brandy. Place persimmon puree in a large mixer bowl, add 1¼ cups sugar and 2 tablespoons butter, and beat together.

3. Sift together flour, baking soda, salt, and spices. Fold the dry ingredients into persimmon puree by hand, mixing well. Add pecans and raisin mixture. Gradually stir in half-and-half, mixing thoroughly.

4. Whip egg whites to soft peaks. Fold them into the pudding and pour into the prepared mold. Secure lid. Tap pudding on counter several times to break up any air bubbles. Carefully lower the mold into the simmering water, placing it in the center of the pot so the steam circulates around the mold. Cover the steam pot. Simmer for 2–2½ hours over low heat, checking to maintain an even water level while steaming the pudding. The pudding is done when a skewer inserted in it comes out almost clean. Cool in pan until pudding shrinks from sides of pan, about 15 minutes. Invert onto serving platter.

5. Prepare Brandy Sauce by melting the butter and sugar together in the top of a double boiler. When melted, cook for an additional minute. Cool slightly. Beat the egg in a small bowl, then whisk it into the melted butter. Whisk in brandy. Either serve immediately or keep warm over hot water.

· · · · · · · ·

NEW YEAR'S AFTERNOON

· · · · · · · ·

Beer-Battered Shrimp and Swiss Cheese Croquettes

Grandma's Cappelletti Soup

Smoked German Dinner with Sauerkraut,
Juniper Berries, and Caraway Seeds

Handmade Chocolate Apple Strudel

· · · · · · · ·

New Year's Day means different things to different people. To some it's a day of resolutions. To others, who celebrated too long the night before, it means a hangover. To football fans it means an orgy of bowl games. The following menu is just what one wants on a lazy afternoon, delighting whoever is sharing the day with you. Since the last thing I've ever felt like doing on New Year's Day is cooking, and you're probably the same, you'll be happy to know that most of this menu can be made ahead of time, so you won't have to miss one touchdown.

BEER-BATTERED SHRIMP AND SWISS CHEESE CROQUETTES

Makes 24, serving 8 as hors d'oeuvres

CROQUETTES
1 quart light German beer
1 cup all-purpose flour
½ pound Swiss cheese, grated (about
  2 cups)
½ teaspoon salt
¼ teaspoon freshly ground black pepper
1 egg yolk
3 tablespoons Dijon mustard
12 cooked small shrimp, cut in half

BEER BATTER
2 cups light German beer
1 cup all-purpose flour
½ teaspoon salt
½ teaspoon paprika
¼ teaspoon freshly ground black pepper
2 tablespoons cornstarch

Oil for frying

1. Prepare croquette dough by pouring beer into a large saucepan. Boil for about 45 minutes, until beer is reduced to 1½ cups. Remove from heat. Add all the flour at once, beating into a thick, fairly dry dough. Add grated cheese, salt, and pepper. Quickly beat in egg yolk. Cool and refrigerate dough overnight.

2. The next day, roll dough into 24 small balls, about 1 inch thick. Make a depression in the center of each ball and put in a touch of mustard and a piece of shrimp. Close dough around filling and again shape into a ball. Set aside or refrigerate until ready to fry. Prepare beer batter in advance by combining all ingredients with a whisk until smooth.

3. To fry, fill a deep pan with 3–4 inches of oil. Heat it to 375°F. Dip the filled croquettes into the beer batter and drop into oil. Fry for several minutes, until brown and cooked through. Drain on paper towels and remove to serving platter.

· · · · · · · ·

GRANDMA'S CAPPELLETTI SOUP

Unquestionably my grandmother Til's most special preparation, her Cappelletti Soup was loved by many people. The roasted meats are ground into a filling for small cappelletti, or pasta "hats," which are then poached and served in a fresh chicken broth. It is quite a tedious task to hand-fold the cappelletti, and you should probably find a helping hand or two. This recipe makes about 180 pieces. Plan on about 12 per person. Fortunately, the tiny cappelletti can be made ahead of time and frozen in a sealed plastic container. Boil as many as you need directly from the freezer without thawing.

Serves 8 (about 180 Cappelletti)

CHICKEN BROTH
1 large boiling chicken, thoroughly
   washed
2 onions, peeled and cut in half
3 carrots, peeled and cut in half
3 stalks celery, washed and cut in half
2 tomatoes, cut in half
2 cloves garlic, peeled
1 bunch parsley stems, thoroughly washed
   and bundled
2 teaspoons salt plus additional to taste
6 black peppercorns
2 teaspoons sugar

MEAT FILLING FOR CAPPELLETTI
(2 CUPS)
½ pound pork shoulder, cut into large
   pieces
½ pound beef chuck or stew meat, cut
   into large pieces
2 eggs, slightly beaten
⅓ cup dry bread crumbs
¼ cup heavy cream
½ teaspoon freshly grated nutmeg
Grated zest from ½ lemon
1½ teaspoons salt plus additional to taste

¼ teaspoon freshly ground black pepper
   plus additional to taste
¼ cup grated Parmesan cheese plus
   additional for serving

1¼ pounds prepared pasta sheets or fresh
   pasta made with 4 eggs, as in
   "Handmade Pasta Dough" (see Index)

1. Place all ingredients for the chicken broth in a large stockpot and fill to top with water. Bring to a simmer, reduce heat, and simmer gently, covered, for 3–4 hours. Taste and add salt if needed. Allow to cool slightly, then remove chicken and vegetables with a slotted spoon; reserve for another use. Strain broth and cool to room temperature. Refrigerate overnight. The next day, remove fat that has accumulated on top. At this point the broth may be refrigerated for up to 4 days or frozen for months.

2. To prepare filling, preheat oven to 375°F and place meats in an uncovered roasting pan. Roast, turning once, until thermometer in pork reads 170°F, about 30 minutes. Remove and use a meat grinder to grind the meats into a large bowl. Add remaining filling ingredients and stir well. Taste and add salt and pepper if needed. Refrigerate until use, overnight if desired.

3. Cut fresh pasta into 1½-inch squares. Put about ¼ teaspoon of filling in the center of each square. Fold the square in half diagonally and seal. Wrap the two points of the long base of the triangle around your fingertip and squeeze them to seal. Place them on a towel to dry. May be air-dried for several hours, then stored in the refrigerator for up to 3 days, or frozen in a sealed container.

4. To cook soup, heat the broth in a large pot until boiling. Add cappelletti and simmer until pasta is cooked, 5–12 minutes after it boils again, depending on how long they were dried. Add water to soup as it evaporates. Divide cappelletti among soup bowls with a slotted spoon; ladle broth over. Serve immediately, passing additional grated Parmesan at the table.

· · · · · · · ·

SMOKED GERMAN DINNER WITH SAUERKRAUT, JUNIPER BERRIES, AND CARAWAY SEEDS

To prepare this dinner, you have to find a neighborhood sausage maker or charcuterie. There you will have at your disposal a selection of products, some smoked, to use in your roasted dinner. You may want to vary the number of meats you use, estimating what each person will be served. You may also want to accompany this dinner with buttered spaetzle noodles or steamed dumplings.

Serves 8

3 pounds spareribs
Salt to taste
Freshly ground black pepper to taste
8 smoked pork chops, 3–4 ounces each
2 quarts sauerkraut, drained
2 tablespoons dark brown sugar
2 tablespoons juniper berries
1 teaspoon caraway seeds
4 würstel or German-style sausages,
   3-4 ounces each
4 small white veal sausages, 3–4 ounces
   each
½ cup hot water

1. Season ribs with salt and black pepper and char spareribs and smoked pork chops on a preheated grill or under a preheated broiler close to heat source for about 10 minutes or until browned. Cut the ribs into two-bone pieces. Oil the bottom of a large roasting pan. Add sauerkraut. Sprinkle with brown sugar, juniper berries, and caraway seeds. Stir lightly to mix. Arrange meat on sauerkraut.

2. Preheat oven to 350°F. Cut an x 1 inch into both ends of the würstel sausages. Arrange on sauerkraut along with remaining sausages. Add hot water, cover, and roast for 1 hour. Stir before serving.

· · · · · · · ·

HANDMADE CHOCOLATE APPLE STRUDEL

My grandmother Til used to stretch her strudel dough by hand and stuff it with a scrumptious blend of fruit, nut, and spice. She called it a *ruchada*, as I still do, though no one ever really knew why. Sometimes during the holidays she would make a filling with pumpkin or my favorite, sautéed spinach and Parmesan. Making the strudels is not as difficult as it sounds. Fortunately they are best if made in advance. The dough-stretching process is something that really should be seen, not written about, but the recipe is just too good not to include.

Makes 2 strudels, about 8 servings each

2 cups all-purpose flour
½ teaspoon salt
¼ cup vegetable oil
10–11 tablespoons water
7–8 green apples
1½ cups sugar
3 teaspoons ground cinnamon
½ cup (¼ pound) unsalted butter, melted
1 cup golden raisins
½ cup packed chopped walnuts
1 teaspoon aniseed
1 ounce unsweetened baking chocolate

1. Using a food processor, combine flour, salt, oil, and enough water to make a soft dough. Allow ball of dough to form in processor and run for 1 minute. By hand, knead for 10–12 minutes, until smooth and elastic. Lightly oil dough, cover with plastic, and allow to rest for 1 hour at room temperature.

2. Meanwhile, peel apples. Core them and cut them into wedges. Slice wedges into ½-inch pieces. You should have 4–5 cups. Combine sugar and cinnamon. Set aside.

3. You will need a large work surface. Use no flour. Cut the dough in half to make two strudels. Your goal is to make an 18″ × 22″ rectangle. Flatten one piece of dough with fingers and stretch it out to a strip, horizontally, about 18 inches wide. Press the dough to the work surface so it adheres and doesn't stretch back. Roll the dough vertically as thin as you can with a rolling pin. Gradually stretch the dough with your fingertips, vertically, beginning at one side and working along the edge, lifting and stretching the dough an inch or 2 at a pass. Adhere it to the work surface as you go. Continue until the rectangle is about 22 inches long. It's all right for a small hole or two to rip. It won't make a difference.

4. Paint the dough with slightly less than half the melted butter. Arrange half the apples over the center of the rectangle, leaving a 1-inch border, and sprinkle evenly with half each of the sugar, raisins, walnuts, and aniseed. Grate half the chocolate over the apples. Roll strudel up starting at bottom edge, little by little, jelly-roll fashion, folding the roll over itself, as you work up the strudel. Twist ends closed. Gently twist the strudel into a spiral shape, trying not to break the skin. Paint a 10-inch pie plate with melted butter, carefully pick up the strudel, and place it in the dish. Paint with butter. Repeat with other strudel. Bake at 375°F for 45 minutes, until golden brown.

5. Remove from oven. Immediately place a dish on top of the strudel and, using oven mitts, invert the strudel onto the plate, allowing the sugary glaze to run over top. Allow to cool to room temperature and wrap in plastic. Refrigerates and freezes well. Serve at room temperature sliced into 2-inch pieces.

· · · · · · · ·

THE PASTA PARTY

. . . .

Classic Antipasto with Crisp Prosciutto Breadsticks

Duck and Spinach Ravioli with Thymed Tomatoes

Sweet Peaches in Burgundy

Tirami Sú with Mascarpone Cheese

Homemade Chocolate Almond Rocca

. . . .

CLASSIC ANTIPASTO

Antipasto means "before the meal," and there are many ways of preparing this classic Italian starter. There is no right or wrong way to make an antipasto, because it should consist of whatever is fresh at the time. In the summer you should include roasted peppers and in the spring perhaps marinated asparagus.

Just outside Rome, on the Appia Antica, there is a restaurant that has an entire wall of antipasti, more than 50 items, and patrons are invited to make their own selection from the enormous variety. At Indigo, I opt for more exotic items than the traditional antipasto spread and have included many of them in this book. The following is a selection of these recipes (see Index for page numbers).

Take into consideration the number of people you're serving; the more people, the greater the variety you can prepare, though it is still most appropriate to serve something as simple as a single salad. Since antipasti are almost always marinated, you can prepare everything in advance. If you don't prepare the breadsticks in this menu, then certainly serve the antipasto with a hot loaf of crusty bread and, of course, a bottle of Italian red wine.

- Malek's Rice-Stuffed Grape Leaves
- Marinated Salt Cod in Garlic and Extra-Virgin Oil
- Papaya and Mango with Honey Lime Dressing
- Roasted Eggplant and Red Onion Salad
- Roasted Red Peppers with Slivered Garlic and Basil
- San Domenico Chicken Liver Pâté

CRISP PROSCIUTTO BREADSTICKS
Makes 32, serving 8

½ cup warm (115°F) water
2 teaspoons honey
2 teaspoons active dry yeast
2 tablespoons extra-virgin olive oil
2 tablespoons semolina flour
2 teaspoons grated Parmesan cheese
½ teaspoon salt
1½ cups bread flour
3 tablespoons finely diced (¼ inch)
   prosciutto
1 egg white, beaten with a pinch of salt

1. To prepare breadstick dough, put warm water in a large electric mixer bowl and stir
   in honey. Add yeast and wait for 5 minutes. Add oil, semolina, Parmesan, salt, and
   bread flour. Using the dough hook attachment, knead at medium-low speed for
   about 5 minutes, until dough is smooth and shiny. Add prosciutto halfway through
   kneading. (Note: This dough may be made by hand following a similar procedure.
   By hand the dough requires about 10 minutes of kneading.)

2. When complete, lightly oil the dough and the mixer bowl. Allow the dough to rise
   in the bowl, covered with a plate, for 1½ hours at room temperature, until doubled.

3. Preheat oven to 425°F. Turn out dough, flatten it to a rectangle, and cut into 16
   sections. Do not use flour. Roll them out to 6-inch lengths, cover with plastic wrap,
   and allow to rest for 20 minutes. Cut sections of dough in half and keep them
   covered. Roll each out to a 15-inch-long strip. Place them lengthwise on baking
   sheets, 1 inch apart. Allow them to rest for 10 minutes, paint with egg white, then
   bake until golden brown, about 12 minutes.

· · · · · · · ·

DUCK AND SPINACH RAVIOLI WITH THYMED TOMATOES

Duck, spinach, tomato, and thyme harmonize with pasta in this special ravioli. If you're having a small party, make the ravioli ahead of time and freeze them. The sauce can be made before guests arrive and reheated after the pasta is boiled. You can vary the meats or vegetables you use in the filling, such as using chicken or escarole instead of duck and spinach.

Serves 4

3 cloves garlic, peeled
4 shallots, peeled
½ pound fresh mushrooms, washed and trimmed
½ pound duck meat, skin removed and reserved
1 10-ounce package frozen chopped spinach
½ cup soft Italian bread crumbs
3 tablespoons light or heavy cream
½ teaspoon salt or to taste
½ teaspoon freshly ground pepper or to taste
2 tablespoons grated Parmesan cheese
¼ teaspoon freshly grated nutmeg
1½ pounds fresh pasta made with 4 eggs, as in "Handmade Pasta Dough" (see Index)

¼ cup extra-virgin olive oil
4 cloves garlic, peeled and sliced fine
Leaves from 1 bunch fresh thyme, chopped
2 pounds Roma-style (plum) tomatoes, peeled and seeded (see Index)
½ teaspoon salt or to taste
½ teaspoon freshly ground black pepper or to taste
Pinch of sugar
2 tablespoons unsalted butter
3 tablespoons grated Parmesan cheese or to taste

1. Put whole garlic cloves in food processor and chop as fine as possible. Add shallots and chop fine. Add mushrooms and chop. Add duck meat and pulse machine until meat is finely chopped. Fry the duck skins in a large skillet until they make about ¼ cup fat. Remove and discard skins. Add duck and mushroom mixture and sauté over medium heat.

2. Meanwhile, boil spinach according to package directions. When finished, strain, rinse with cold water, and squeeze until very dry. When meat mixture is almost dry, remove to a large bowl and add spinach, bread crumbs, cream, salt, pepper, 2 tablespoons Parmesan, and nutmeg. Mix lightly and refrigerate or freeze for later use.

3. Cut pasta sheets into 2-inch squares. Paint rim with water, place a small ball of filling in center, cover with another sheet, press out air, and seal. Cut out with a

round cookie cutter or an inverted glass. Set on a kitchen towel and air-dry until time to cook. They may also be air-dried for several hours and then frozen.

4. Heat olive oil in a large saucepan. Add garlic and cook slowly until tender, not brown, about 5 minutes. Turn heat to high and add chopped thyme, tomatoes, salt, pepper, and a pinch of sugar. Sauté tomatoes quickly; after only a minute or 2, turn off heat. Add butter and mash garlic with a fork.

5. Boil ravioli in salted water for about 4 minutes (longer if frozen) after water returns to a boil. Remove them with a slotted spoon and add to saucepan with the tomatoes. Turn heat to medium and cook lightly for another minute. Add 3 tablespoons Parmesan and stir. Allow to sit for 2 minutes before serving. Arrange on individual plates or one large platter.

· · · · · · · ·

SWEET PEACHES IN BURGUNDY

This is a simple old Italian tradition, sweet peaches served in red wine to finish a meal. There is nothing more to the dish than that, except that both ingredients must be of superb quality. Peaches hit peak season during July and August, and if your pasta party is in the summer, you will have a wonderful selection from which to choose. If there's snow on the sidewalk for your dinner party, you may change fruit, using crisp winter pears instead of peaches. The better-tasting the wine, the more splendid this after-dinner refresher becomes. To prepare this dish, wash one peach per person. Cut the peaches in half and remove pits. Slice each peach into eight wedges. Place them in goblets and pour about ½ cup wine over each.

TIRAMI SU WITH MASCARPONE CHEESE

Almost every restaurant in Italy serves its own unique version of tirami sú, which means "pick me up" to the Italians. Considering the coffee and sugar in this glorious dessert, it does just that. This version was inspired by one of the restaurants in whose pastry kitchen I worked. Every morning the day's tirami sú was assembled, to be set on display that evening in the dining room. As it was ordered, large scoops were spooned out and served on chilled plates. Mascarpone is a type of Italian cheese made by thickening heavy cream with an acid similar to cream of tartar, resulting in something best compared to the cream cheese we make in Philadelphia. It has the natural sweetness of cream and, though sometimes eaten by itself, is most often used in Italian pastries. Your local Italian market probably imports this divine cheese, but if you must, you can substitute ½ pound ricotta cheese and 1 cup heavy cream, whipped together until smooth in a food processor. You must know, however, as with everything, that the final product will be best with the real thing.

Serves 6

1 cup strong brewed espresso coffee, cooled
3 tablespoons Kahlúa
12 ladyfingers, lightly toasted in a 375°F oven for 15 minutes
3 tablespoons plus 1 teaspoon sugar
3 eggs, separated

2 teaspoons brandy
½ pound imported Mascarpone cheese
¼ cup cold whipping cream
3 ounces bittersweet chocolate, chopped fine
Unsweetened cocoa powder for dusting

1. Combine the cold coffee with the Kahlúa. Arrange half the ladyfingers in one layer on the bottom of an oval serving dish and lightly soak them with the coffee and Kahlúa mixture.

2. In a small double boiler on top of a simmering water bath, combine 3 tablespoons sugar, egg yolks, and brandy, whipping by hand until the sugar dissolves and the egg yolks become light. Remove from heat and add Mascarpone. Stir lightly to incorporate.

3. Whip the egg whites until they are stiff, adding a teaspoon of sugar at midpoint. Gently fold the egg whites into the Mascarpone mixture. Then whip the cream in a small chilled bowl until thick and fold it as well into the Mascarpone mixture.

4. Spoon half of this mixture on top of the ladyfingers. Sprinkle with half the chocolate. Repeat with another layer of ladyfingers, soak with coffee, then spoon on remaining Mascarpone mixture and chocolate. Smooth top and dust with cocoa. Refrigerate until serving time.

· · · · · · · ·

HOMEMADE CHOCOLATE ALMOND ROCCA

A scoop of tirami sú, a decorated plate of this glorious chocolate almond rocca, and a rich cup of dark roast Italian coffee is the only way to wind up your pasta party.

1 cup (½ pound) plus 2 tablespoons
    unsalted butter, softened
2 cups shelled almonds
1⅓ cups sugar
1 tablespoon light corn syrup
3 tablespoons water
1 pound semisweet chocolate

1. Preheat oven to 375°F. Heavily rub the bottom and sides of a 13″ × 9″ baking sheet with the 2 tablespoons butter. Set aside. Toast nuts on a cookie sheet until lightly brown, stirring once. Cool slightly and chop half of them coarse and half of them fine. Set aside.

2. Melt 1 cup butter in a large saucepan. Add sugar, corn syrup, and water. Cook, stirring often, until a candy thermometer registers 300°F. Watch it carefully after 280°F, as it increases quickly. At 300°F, quickly stir in coarsely chopped nuts and spread in the buttered baking sheet. Allow to cool.

3. Meanwhile, melt the chocolate in the top of a double boiler or in a microwave. Turn the candy out onto a large sheet of wax paper. Spread the top with half the chocolate and sprinkle with half the finely chopped nuts. Press them in lightly. Lay another sheet of wax paper over top and flip the slab over. Repeat with remaining chocolate and nuts. Chill until firm, then break into pieces. Store the candy in a closed container in a cool place, not in the refrigerator.

· · · · · · · ·

TRADITIONS

Passing down recipes within a family is an age-old tradition. They are sometimes scratched on paper, sometimes simply committed to memory. These menus offer a sampling of ethnic specialties and have become favorites in many cultures.

MEDITERRANEAN SUNSHINE

········

Malek's Rice-Stuffed Grape Leaves

Bouillabaisse of Baby Calamari,
Tomato, and Olive Oil on Crusty Croutons

Baby Lamb Chops Roasted with Garlic and Rosemary

Broccoli Custards

Honey Mousse with Candied Pine Nuts

········

MALEK'S RICE-STUFFED GRAPE LEAVES

Years ago I worked with a man from the Middle East who taught me to make these incredible stuffed grape leaves among other traditional specialties. They require quite a bit of time and hand work but are well worth their toll. To serve, arrange the stuffed leaves on a platter with a bowl of Greek-style Kalamata olives and crumbled feta cheese, first tossed with some extra-virgin olive oil, oregano, and fresh squeezed lemon. They keep well in the refrigerator and are best served at room temperature.

Makes 90 Stuffed Grape Leaves

    1 red onion, peeled and diced very fine
    1 tablespoon salt
    1½ teaspoons freshly ground black pepper
    1 teaspoon ground cinnamon
    Juice of 1 lemon (about 3 tablespoons)
    1 pound Arborio (short-grain) rice
    1¼ cups extra-virgin olive oil
    Leaves from 2–3 bunches Italian (flat-leaf)
      parsley, washed and chopped fine
      (about 4 cups)
    4 firm ripe tomatoes, diced very fine
    Leaves from 1 bunch fresh mint, washed
      and chopped fine (about ½ cup)
    1 8-ounce jar grape leaves
    2 large tomatoes, sliced ½ inch thick

1. Prepare filling by placing diced onion in a bowl. Add 2 teaspoons of the salt, the pepper, and the cinnamon. Add lemon juice and rice. Mix and add 1 cup of the olive oil. Add parsley, tomatoes, and mint. Allow to set for 30 minutes or overnight. Mix well before using.

2. Wash grape leaves in cold water. Fill leaf by laying leaf flat on counter, stem side up. Place 1 heaped tablespoon of filling at bottom in center of leaf, just above stem. Fold bottom of leaf over filling, fold in sides, then roll up tightly. It should be about 1″ × 2″.

3. Arrange tomato slices over bottom of a large, straight-sided saucepan. Add remaining ¼ cup olive oil. Stack leaves tightly in pan on tomatoes. Cover top of the bundles with several opened grape leaves. Pour the juices left over from the rice filling into a measuring cup and add water to make 2 cups; pour over leaves. Lay a dinner plate on top to act as a weight. Cover.

4. Bring to a boil, then simmer for 1¼ hours, until rice is tender, adding additional water as necessary. Remove from heat and allow to cool. The cooked tomato on the bottom may be used to garnish the leaves. Grape leaves keep in the refrigerator for at least 1 week.

• • • • • • • •

BOUILLABAISSE OF BABY CALAMARI, TOMATO, AND OLIVE OIL ON CRUSTY CROUTONS

On the Italian Riviera tender calamari is poached in fish broth with herbs and is served on crisp, garlicky croutons. It differs from the classic bouillabaisse in that it more closely resembles a soup than a stew, not containing great assortments of seafood and other typical ingredients. You'll find it is light and flavorful, an ideal beginning to your menu.

Serves 4

4 thick slices crusty French or Italian bread
2 cloves garlic, peeled
¼ cup extra-virgin olive oil
¼ cup olive oil
1 small onion, peeled and diced
6 cloves garlic, peeled and sliced thin
1 cup homemade fish broth or bottled clam juice
¼ cup dry white wine
¼ cup dry sherry
¼ cup coarsely chopped Italian (flat-leaf) parsley

Pinch of hot red pepper flakes (optional)
½ teaspoon ground fennel seed
5 Roma-style (plum) tomatoes, peeled and seeded (see Index)
4 fresh basil leaves
1¼ pounds cleaned baby squid (See Crisp Fried Baby Calamari and Smelts)
3 tablespoons unsalted butter
Salt to taste
Freshly ground black pepper to taste

1. Preheat broiler and toast bread on both sides. Rub with whole garlic cloves. Arrange bread slices in bowls and drizzle each with 1 tablespoon extra-virgin olive oil.

2. In a large, heavy stockpot, heat ¼ cup olive oil and sauté onion until it begins to color; add garlic. Cook for a moment, then add fish broth, white wine, sherry, parsley, hot red pepper flakes, and fennel seed. Cover and simmer for 10 minutes, until it becomes a rich, thick stock.

3. Turn heat to high and add tomatoes, basil, and squid. Cook until squid is just tender, about 2 minutes after it simmers again. Add butter and salt and pepper to taste. Do not overcook, as squid will toughen. Spoon squid over croutons and fill bowls with broth.

· · · · · · · ·

150

BABY LAMB CHOPS
ROASTED WITH GARLIC AND ROSEMARY

You can purchase whole racks of baby lamb from your butcher. They almost always contain eight rib bones and modestly serve two people. Garlic and rosemary bushes abound throughout the Mediterranean area, and in no greater way has lamb ever been perfumed. This dish requires some last-minute cooking, so plan your meal around it. Everything should be done and ready to go when the chops are just medium-rare.

Serves 4

2 racks of baby lamb, 8 bones per rack,
   trimmed of fat
Salt to taste
Freshly ground black pepper to taste
3 tablespoons olive oil
3 tablespoons thinly sliced garlic, cut
   lengthwise
3 fresh rosemary stems, each about 8
   inches long, cut into 2-inch pieces
½ cup dry red wine
3 tablespoons unsalted butter, softened

1. Preheat oven to 400°F. Cut each rack of lamb into four pieces, two ribs per piece. Sprinkle each chop with salt and pepper on both sides. Put olive oil in a large, heavy skillet or dutch oven, tilting to coat pan. Place over medium-high heat; when oil is almost smoking hot, add chops and sear on one side.

2. Flip chops and arrange sliced garlic and rosemary between chops. Place skillet in the oven and roast chops, uncovered, for 7–9 minutes for medium-rare and a few minutes longer if you prefer medium-well. Flip them around after the bottoms have seared. Do not overcook.

3. Remove from oven and place on burner already set to high; add red wine. Toss chops in wine; remove rosemary stems. Add butter and continue to turn chops until wine is almost gone and all that's left is a thin sauce. Remove from heat and place two chops on each plate or put all on one large serving platter. Add any juices that have accumulated to the skillet, then strain sauce and spoon over chops. Garnish with a sprig of the cooked rosemary.

· · · · · · · ·

BROCCOLI CUSTARDS

These custards are a common sight in elegant European restaurants. They can be made with almost any vegetable, from asparagus to spinach, and always make an impressive side dish. Be careful that the water bath never gets too hot, or the custard may break and become grainy.

Serves 4

1 bunch broccoli
2 tablespoons unsalted butter, softened
1 cup half-and-half
3 large eggs, slightly beaten
¼ teaspoon freshly grated nutmeg
¼ teaspoon freshly ground white pepper
1 tablespoon grated Parmesan cheese
½ teaspoon salt or to taste

1. Remove the small flowerets from broccoli, trimming them to 1½ inches. Steam them (or microwave them for 6–7 minutes on HIGH with a bit of water) until quite tender. Drain on paper towels and allow to cool. Grease 4 6-ounce custard cups or soufflé ramekins with 2 tablespoons butter.

2. Prepare custard by blending remaining ingredients in a bowl. Preheat oven to 325°F. Roughly mash 1 cup of the cooked broccoli with a fork and add to custard. Arrange broccoli flowerets vertically, stems upward, in custard cups.

3. Fill cups with the custard mixture. Place them in a baking pan and add hot water to come halfway up sides of cups. Place water bath in the oven. Cook for 35–45 minutes or until set. When a knife inserted in the center comes out clean, custard is set. Remove from water bath, cool for 5 minutes, loosen the sides with a butter knife, and invert onto plates. Custards may be reheated in the microwave for a moment before serving.

· · · · · · · ·

HONEY MOUSSE WITH CANDIED PINE NUTS

This smooth, honey-flavored mousse is accented by crunchy candied pine nuts and serves as a light and unique dessert. You can spoon the mousse into stemmed glasses or small ramekins or serve one large bowl, spooning it out at the table along with hot coffee. The candied nuts are addictive and also quite versatile; you may therefore want to double or triple the recipe for them. Store unused nuts in a closed container at room temperature. They stay fresh for a week or so.

Serves 6

2 teaspoons water
¼ cup sugar
¾ cup pine nuts
3 egg yolks
⅓ cup honey
½ cup whipping cream
Additional pine nuts for garnish

1. Candy the pine nuts by combining the water and sugar in a small saucepan. Bring to a boil and add nuts. Stir constantly with a wooden spoon over medium-high heat until water evaporates and sugar becomes granular. Continue to stir until nuts begin to turn light golden. Do not allow sugar to caramelize. Immediately dump onto a metal baking sheet; break them apart as they cool.

2. Prepare mousse by whipping egg yolks and honey until thick and pale, about 10 minutes. Set aside. Whip cream until soft peaks form.

3. Fold egg yolk/honey mixture into cream just until thoroughly combined. Fold in 1 cup of the candied pine nuts. Spoon mousse into individual serving dishes and freeze for at least 2 hours. Allow to sit at room temperature for 15 minutes before serving. Garnish with additional pine nuts. May be frozen for up to 3 days.

· · · · · · · ·

SOUTHWESTERN FARE

· · · · · · · ·

Santa Fe Grilled Vegetable Salad with Lemon-Cilantro Vinaigrette

Chili-Rubbed Chicken and Soft Tortillas

Green Tomatillo Salsa

Sweet Corn and Red Pepper Fritters

Carmen Miranda Fruit Salad

· · · · · · · ·

SANTA FE GRILLED VEGETABLE SALAD WITH LEMON-CILANTRO VINAIGRETTE

The vegetables in this salad are marinated in garlic and seasonings, then grilled and chilled, later to be tossed with a sprightly lemon dressing. At Indigo we serve the vegetables on salad greens that are tossed with the same dressing, then garnished with some fresh fried blue corn tortilla chips. If you plan to heat oil to fry the corn and pepper fritters later in this menu, first use the oil to fry a few tortilla strips or chips. If not, packaged are fine. Choose as large an assortment of vegetables as possible, basing your selection on color and texture.

Serves 4

¼ cup olive oil

4 cloves garlic, peeled and put through a garlic press

1 teaspoon salt or to taste

½ teaspoon freshly ground black pepper or to taste

1 teaspoon sugar

1 red bell pepper, seeded and cut into 8 pieces

1 zucchini, cut in half lengthwise, then cut in half crosswise

2 yellow crookneck squash, cut in half lengthwise

1 small bunch broccoli, cut into 3-inch pieces

2 small red onions, peeled and cut in half

8 mushrooms, skewered for grilling

2 carrots, peeled, sliced in half lengthwise, then cut in half crosswise

2 cups assorted salad greens

Lemon-Cilantro Vinaigrette (recipe follows)

Blue corn tortilla chips and cilantro sprigs for garnish

1. Make vegetable marinade by combining the olive oil, garlic, salt, pepper, and sugar in a small bowl; stir until dissolved. Place all vegetables except salad greens in a large bowl. Add marinade, toss well, and refrigerate until grilling time, at least 1 hour.

2. Preheat grill to medium-high heat. Arrange vegetables on grate. In about 5 minutes, once grill marks are made, carefully turn the vegetables, taking care that they don't fall through the grate. Since they all cook at different rates, you must monitor the grill, removing them as they are lightly charred and beginning to soften. They will continue to cook after being removed from the heat. As they finish, place them on a platter and refrigerate until chilled.

3. At serving time, toss some assorted greens in a bowl with the vinaigrette. Arrange on plates. Toss vegetables with additional vinaigrette and arrange on top of the salad. Garnish with blue corn tortilla chips and cilantro sprigs.

LEMON-CILANTRO VINAIGRETTE
Makes about 1 cup

5 scallions, white parts only
3 cloves garlic, peeled
Leaves from 1 bunch cilantro (about
    ½ cup)
Grated zest from 1 lemon
Juice and pulp from 1 lemon, seeds
    removed
1 teaspoon sugar
1 tablespoon rice wine vinegar
½ teaspoon salt or to taste
½ teaspoon freshly ground black pepper
    or to taste
½ cup extra-virgin olive oil

Combine all ingredients in a blender and puree until smooth. Taste and correct seasonings; the dressing should be quite robust. Thin with a little water if necessary. The dressing is best when made the day before you plan to use it.

· · · · · · · ·

CHILI-RUBBED CHICKEN AND SOFT TORTILLAS

An exciting combination of southwestern flavors explodes from this whole roasted chicken. If you're cooking for many people, you can apply the same chili butter to chicken pieces, then roast them on a rack on a baking sheet until brown and crispy. I always make extra—it's an exceptional leftover as is or can be baked into an enchilada torta (see Index). The robust chicken is traditionally eaten in small pieces rolled up in steaming tortillas oozing with tomatillo salsa. Have something chocolate around for the end of the meal—everyone always seems to crave it.

Serves 4

6 tablespoons unsalted butter, softened
1 heaped teaspoon cumin seed
1 heaped teaspoon ground coriander
1 heaped teaspoon paprika
1 heaped teaspoon mild chili powder
Heaped ½ teaspoon ground cinnamon
2 tablespoons fresh lime juice
1 jalapeño chili
2 teaspoons salt plus additional to taste
4 cloves garlic, peeled
1 2-inch piece of fresh gingerroot, peeled
1 large chicken, about 3 pounds, washed
　well
12 flour tortillas

1. In a small bowl, combine the butter, cumin, coriander, paprika, chili powder, cinnamon, and lime juice. Mix well. Using a knife or food processor, mince together the remaining seasonings, then whip into the butter.

2. Place chicken on rack in baking pan, breast up. Rub chili butter thoroughly over entire inside and outside of chicken, rubbing flavors into the meat. Allow to marinate for several hours in refrigerator.

3. Two hours before serving, preheat oven to 375°F and sprinkle chicken with salt. Slowly roast chicken for about 2 hours, until skin is crisp and juices run clear, depending on size of chicken. Tent with foil during baking after chicken becomes golden. When finished, remove from oven and allow to rest for 15–20 minutes before carving. Separate legs and thigh and cut breast into four pieces. Serve with warmed flour tortillas and Green Tomatillo Salsa (recipe follows).

· · · · · · · ·

156

GREEN TOMATILLO SALSA

Every southwestern restaurant and cook has its own special way of making tomatillo salsa. This is a combination of several recipes and is my favorite. It keeps only for a day, then it loses its bright green color and fresh texture.

Makes 2 cups

>5 tomatillos, husks removed, chopped
>   coarse
>2 cloves garlic, peeled and chopped
>   coarse
>Leaves from ½ bunch cilantro (about
>   ¼ cup)
>1 small jalapeño chili or to taste, sliced
>4 scallions, 2 inches trimmed from tops,
>   cut into pieces
>Juice of 1 lime
>1 teaspoon sugar
>½ teaspoon salt or to taste
>½ teaspoon freshly ground black pepper
>   or to taste

Place all ingredients in a food processor. Chop until minced fine but not pureed. Taste and add salt and pepper if necessary. Let salsa rest for an hour before serving to allow flavors to develop.

· · · · · · · ·

SWEET CORN AND RED PEPPER FRITTERS

The sweet corn and the crunchy red peppers provide great taste and texture in these special fritters. If you must fry them ahead of time, keep them on a baking sheet, then warm them for a few minutes in a hot oven. If the spicy chicken and spicy salsa aren't enough for you, you can always add some chopped chilies to the batter.

Makes 12, serving 4

1 ear sweet corn, shucked
½ red bell pepper, seeded
¾ cup all-purpose flour
¾ teaspoon baking powder
¼ teaspoon baking soda
⅛ teaspoon freshly grated nutmeg
Pinch of salt
2 teaspoons sugar
1 egg
3–4 tablespoons milk
1 tablespoon minced cilantro leaves
Vegetable oil for frying

1. Remove kernels from ear of corn by standing ear upright and cutting downward with a sharp knife. Reserve in a bowl. Cut pepper into ¼-inch dice and combine with corn.

2. Mix together the flour, baking powder, soda, nutmeg, salt, and sugar. Beat egg until frothy. Add milk and all dry ingredients. Blend well. Stir in corn, peppers, and cilantro. Fritter batter should resemble thick pancake batter; if it's too thick, add some milk.

3. Fill a deep pan with 3 inches of vegetable oil. Heat to 350°F. Begin dropping in the batter by the generous tablespoonful and fry for 2–3 minutes, until golden. Remove to paper towels and keep fritters warm while frying remaining batter. Serve warm. May be reheated in the oven.

· · · · · · · ·

CARMEN MIRANDA FRUIT SALAD

For anyone too young to recall who Carmen Miranda was, she played a huge role in the movies of the 1940s and was known as "The Lady in the Tutti-Frutti Hat." Because she wore what seemed to be a bushel of fruit on her head, it seemed only fitting to dedicate this salad to her.

It is really not necessary to follow a recipe for fruit salad. What you need to end up with, for four or five people, is one quart of fresh fruit, cut and peeled with care. Prepare a combination of the freshest seasonal fruit you can find—cantaloupe should be in small, even pieces; the orange sections should have no white pith; peel the pears but not the apples. Everything should be bite-size—whole red and green grapes, strawberry halves, kiwifruit slices, pitted black cherries, fresh coconut, banana slices rinsed with lemon juice. Now add 1 tablespoon honey, ¼ cup tequila, 1 tablespoon fresh lime juice, and ¼ cup apple or orange juice. Mix well and refrigerate until serving time. Olé!

· · · · · · · ·

FRENCH BISTRO

. . . .

Chilled Beaujolais Nouveau

Alsatian Onion and Oxtail Soup Gratinée

*Niçoise Salad with Grilled Fresh Tuna, Haricots Verts, Baby Pink
Potatoes, Hard-Cooked Egg, and Provençal Olives*

Almond Tart with Prune Sauce

. . . .

CHILLED BEAUJOLAIS NOUVEAU

Beaujolais is now one of the most widely enjoyed red wines in the world. It is a wine to be taken young and to be drunk, not sipped. Nowadays it is fermented very quickly, depending on the maturity achieved on the vine in a particular summer, and this is why it is light, fruity, and flowery.

Tasters sometimes say they detect the taste or scent of peach, apricot, or rose in the wine, but whatever the individual may find, it will always be the flower and fruit and freshness that will give it distinction and beauty. This is why one drinks Beaujolais young, usually under three years. Most of it is red, made from the Gamay grape, although there is some excellent white Beaujolais, Beaujolais Blanc, that is made from the Chardonnay.

The French district that grows the grape is situated between Mâcon and Lyons in southern Burgundy, where the land is very hilly and the soil is rich in granite. It produces a wine that is light in alcohol and doesn't travel well, some of which is drunk from the barrel and only rarely bottled. When drunk from the barrel, the wine has a tremendous fruity taste, something I will always remember.

In the United States and abroad somewhat of a fad for drinking the very young wine, Beaujolais Nouveau, has developed. Though the vintners of Burgundy see it just as the wine they happen to be drinking around the end of the vintage year, many others rush to get the first of the bottling. To prepare for this hurried bottling, it must be racked and reracked both to remove sediment that would normally have time to settle out naturally and to prevent a sour fermentation. In the process the very heart of Beaujolais is poured away. It is one of the few red wines that tastes best when chilled. Pour generously.

ALSATIAN ONION AND OXTAIL SOUP GRATINEE

This fragrant soup is enjoyed late at night and into the small hours of the morning at almost every bistro throughout France. In Alsace the beef stock with which the soup is prepared is simmered with oxtails, giving the soup its extraordinary flavor. You can request beef oxtails from your local butcher; have him or her saw them into two-inch sections for you. Make sure you cook the onions slowly so they attain a caramel color without charring and becoming bitter. The combination of cheeses used to make the soup gratinée has a unique purpose, adding flavor, color, and the characteristic "stretchiness" of cheese.

Serves 4

2½ pounds beef oxtails, cut into small pieces

2 quarts water

3 carrots, peeled and cut in half

2 stalks celery, cut into large pieces

2 cloves garlic, peeled

2 sprigs fresh thyme

4 sprigs Italian (flat-leaf) parsley

1 teaspoon salt plus additional to taste

4 black peppercorns

5 tablespoons unsalted butter

1 pound onions, peeled and sliced thin (2–2½ cups)

1 tablespoon all-purpose flour

½ cup Beaujolais

3 ounces Gruyère or Emmenthaler cheese, grated (¾ cup)

2 ounces mozzarella cheese, grated (½ cup)

2 tablespoons grated Parmesan cheese

4 1-inch-thick slices French bread

1. Begin the day before serving by preparing the beef broth. Combine the oxtails with the water in a stockpot. Bring to a simmer and add carrots, celery, garlic, herbs, salt, and peppercorns. Simmer for 2–3 hours, covered. Strain the broth into a saucepan; season with additional salt to taste. Remove meat from the oxtails and dice into ¼-inch pieces to make 1 cup. Refrigerate soup and meat overnight.

2. The next day, remove fat from soup and bring to a simmer. Melt the butter in a large saucepan. Add the onions and cook over medium-low heat, stirring often, for 25 minutes, until they become soft and golden brown. Sprinkle in the flour and cook for another couple of minutes. Remove from heat and add the hot beef broth; stir to dissolve the flour. Return to the heat, add wine and reserved diced meat, cover, and simmer for 45 minutes.

3. Preheat broiler. Combine all cheeses in a bowl. Toast the slices of bread on both sides under the broiler. Divide them among four flameproof soup bowls. Fill each bowl with the soup. Arrange cheese over top and slide them under the broiler, close to the heat source, broiling just long enough to lightly brown the cheese. Serve immediately.

· · · · · · · ·

NIÇOISE SALAD WITH GRILLED FRESH TUNA, HARICOTS VERTS, BABY PINK POTATOES, HARD-COOKED EGG, AND PROVENÇAL OLIVES

There are many versions of the distinguished Niçoise salad, and here is one more. This uses fresh tuna, the way it was in the beginning, before cans. At Indigo we marinate the tuna with some herbs, then sear it on the grill, since it's always hot and ready for use. At home firing up charcoal can be bothersome for a piece of tuna, so if you prefer you can just sear it in a little olive oil until it's charred on each side, making sure it doesn't overcook.

Serves 4

3 tablespoons olive oil
2 cloves garlic, peeled and minced or put through a press
2 teaspoons minced fresh thyme or rosemary leaves *or* 1 teaspoon dried
2 8-ounce slices fresh Ahi or albacore tuna, cut in half
Salt to taste
Freshly ground pepper to taste
4 eggs, hard-cooked
4 pink new potatoes, well scrubbed

1 pound assorted salad greens, with added Italian (flat-leaf) parsley leaves
1 pound haricots verts or small green beans
Balsamic Vinaigrette (see Index) or other vinaigrette
¼ cup small black Provençal olives
4 small tomatoes, diced
4 canned anchovy fillets, rinsed under cold water (optional)
8 roasted red pepper strips (optional)

1. In a small bowl, combine the olive oil, garlic, and herbs. Sprinkle the tuna with salt and pepper and coat the sides with the marinade. Allow to rest for 30 minutes while you prepare the salad.

2. Peel and quarter the hard-cooked eggs. Boil potatoes in salted water until tender, about 10–12 minutes, drain and cool; slice them thin. Wash and dry salad greens and refrigerate them. Boil the green beans in salted water until just tender, about 3–5 minutes. Drain, rinse with cold water, and refrigerate. Grill the tuna quickly over high heat to sear each side; it should still be pink in the center. Set aside.

3. To assemble salad, toss the greens with a little of the vinaigrette. Arrange on plates. On top of the salad greens, arrange in groups the tuna, eggs, potatoes, haricots verts, olives, tomatoes, anchovies, and pepper strips. Drizzle additional dressing in a circle over the top and serve.

· · · · · · · ·

ALMOND TART WITH PRUNE SAUCE

I first savored this almond tart in a faded little bistro outside of Lyons, France. The tart is not too sweet and is served with a luscious prune sauce.

Serves 4–6 (1 9-inch tart)

1½ cups all-purpose flour, sifted
1 cup sugar
¾ cup (6 ounces) unsalted butter, chilled
⅓ cup milk
1½ cups blanched slivered almonds,
    ground fine

4 eggs, lightly beaten
½ cup milk
1 teaspoon vanilla extract
Prune Sauce (recipe follows)
Grated orange zest for garnish

1. Butter a 9-inch tart pan. Preheat oven to 375°F. Place flour and 3 tablespoons of the sugar in a food processor. Cut butter into slices and add; pulse machine to cut butter through flour until it's like small peas. Add ⅓ cup milk by the tablespoon, pulsing the machine just enough to make the dough cohere. Chill for several minutes, then roll out about ¼ inch thick. Line tart pan with dough and chill.

2. In a food processor, process the almonds with ¾ cup sugar until ground. Add eggs, ½ cup milk, and vanilla. Process until smooth and as thick as heavy cream. Pour into tart shell and bake for 15 minutes. Reduce heat to 350°F and bake for another 15 minutes. Sprinkle remaining tablespoon of sugar on tart and bake for 2 minutes more. Allow to cool in tart pan for at least 30 minutes. The tart is best chilled overnight. Spoon Prune Sauce onto plates and place servings of tart on top. Garnish with a pinch of orange zest.

PRUNE SAUCE
Makes 1½ cups

½ cup sugar
1 cup water
½ pound pitted prunes
½ teaspoon fresh lemon juice

1. Combine sugar and water in a saucepan and boil until sugar melts. Add prunes and simmer for 20 minutes. Cover the pan and allow fruit to sit for 15 minutes.

2. Puree the prunes and their liquid in a food processor. Set a strainer over another saucepan and add the prune puree. Press through with a rubber spatula. Add lemon juice. Thin to sauce consistency with water as necessary and stir before using.

· · · · · · · ·

SUNDAY SOUL

. . . .

Skillet Corn Bread

Crisp Southern-Fried Paprika Chicken

Black-Eyed Peas and Braised Cabbage

Mississippi Mud Pie

. . . .

SKILLET CORN BREAD

There are as many recipes for corn bread as there are pecan trees in the South. This happens to be my favorite, shown to me by a southern friend, the way her mother used to make it. I love the idea of baking and serving the bread in a black skillet, which adds not only an authentic touch of the South but also a crisp, buttery crust on the bottom and sides. You may add all sort of things to your corn bread, from cheddar cheese to corn to jalapeño peppers, though I still think it's best plain.

Makes 1 10-inch corn bread, serving 4–6

⅓ cup all-purpose flour
1½ cups yellow cornmeal
1½ teaspoons baking powder
½ teaspoon salt
2 eggs
1 cup buttermilk
2 cups milk
2 tablespoons unsalted butter

1. Preheat the oven to 350°F. Sift together all dry ingredients into a large bowl. Beat eggs until light and foamy and stir them into flour mixture. Add buttermilk and 1 cup of the milk and blend to form a batter.

2. Heat butter in a 9-inch black cast-iron skillet over medium heat until it sizzles. Tilt pan to grease bottom and sides. While still hot, pour batter into skillet and evenly drizzle remaining cup of milk on top, without stirring. Immediately place skillet in oven and bake for about 50 minutes, until brown and set. Slice into wedges before serving.

. . . .

CRISP SOUTHERN-FRIED PAPRIKA CHICKEN

This is the way they love to eat chicken in the South—simple and crisp. There are two secrets to this dish. The first is the marinade. The buttermilk contains lactic acid, which serves as a tenderizer and a flavor enhancer. The second is allowing the flour to dry on the chicken. If you bread or flour anything and fry it immediately, the breading has a tendency to fall off during frying. Allowing it to dry for 30 minutes or so will ensure a perfect, crispy coating. You can buy precut chicken parts for this; however, in the South a whole bird is always chopped up.

Serves 4

1 large chicken, about 3 pounds
2 cups buttermilk
1 heaped tablespoon Hungarian paprika
Approximately 8 dashes of Tabasco sauce
2 cups all-purpose flour
2 teaspoons salt
1 heaped teaspoon freshly ground black
    pepper
Peanut oil for frying

1. Using a sharp knife, carefully remove and discard (or reserve for stock) back of chicken. Cut leg quarters off chicken, always cutting through a joint, not a bone. Separate thighs from legs. Remove breastbone and separate breast in two. Remove wing sections from breasts. You should have eight pieces. Wash pieces well. Dry with paper towels.

2. Combine buttermilk, paprika, and Tabasco in a large bowl; add chicken parts. Marinate in refrigerator for at least 1 hour; up to 4 hours is best.

3. Put the flour into a plastic bag large enough to contain chicken. Add salt and pepper. Mix flour in bag, then toss chicken thoroughly, squeezing to adhere flour to each piece. Air-dry the chicken parts on a rack for 30 minutes.

4. In a large, heavy skillet, heat 1 inch of oil over high heat until hot. Add chicken pieces and reduce heat slightly. Fry moderately for 15 minutes; chicken should be brown and crisp on the bottom before you turn it. Then turn and cook for 10–15 minutes more, removing breast pieces first. Lower heat if chicken is browning too quickly before cooking time is up. Medium heat is usually just right. Remove to rack and allow to cool slightly before serving.

· · · · · · · ·

BLACK-EYED PEAS AND BRAISED CABBAGE

Black-eyed peas are considered a staple in almost all southern households, something that's always available to be cooked with fatback or hog jowls, served up with collard greens or braised cabbage. They can be prepared entirely ahead of time and served at room temperature, family style, along with the cabbage, when the chicken is done.

Serves 4

¼ pound sliced bacon, cut into ¼-inch
  julienne
1 small onion, peeled and minced
1 stalk celery, minced, with some leaves
4 cloves garlic, peeled and minced
2 pinches of hot red pepper flakes or to
  taste
1 cup (about 7 ounces) dried black-eyed
  peas, rinsed and picked over
2 teaspoons cider vinegar
3 cups chicken broth
½ teaspoon salt or to taste
Approximately 2 cups water
1 head green cabbage, cored and sliced
  into ¼-inch shreds
1 teaspoon sugar

1. In a large saucepan, fry half the bacon over medium heat until it begins to brown; add onion and celery and continue to cook for a few more minutes, until wilted. Add half the garlic, then a pinch of hot red pepper, the black-eyed peas, and the vinegar. Sauté for a moment longer, then add 2 cups of the chicken broth and the salt. Cover and simmer for 40 minutes. Add 1 cup water and simmer for another 40 minutes. Add remaining cup of water and simmer for 20 minutes, until peas are tender, adding more water as necessary, stirring occasionally. When done, season with salt to taste and set aside. There should be very little liquid in the pan, but the peas should not be dry.

2. Just before serving or after peas are cooked, prepare cabbage by rendering remaining bacon in a large pot. When brown and crispy, add a pinch of red pepper flakes and remaining garlic. Cook for a moment, then add cabbage, sugar, and remaining cup chicken broth. Cover and steam the cabbage until tender, stirring occasionally, about 8 minutes. Season with salt.

3. Add the peas to the cabbage and toss well. Arrange in a large bowl and serve hot. May be made in advance and served at room temperature.

· · · · · · · ·

MISSISSIPPI MUD PIE

This twist on an old southern favorite replaces the traditional flaky crust with a spicy gingersnap crust.

Makes 1 10-inch pie, serving 12

1⅓ cups gingersnap cookie crumbs (about 25 cookies)
1½ cups plus 2 tablespoons sugar
½ teaspoon ground cinnamon
⅓ cup unsalted butter, melted
½ cup (¼ pound) unsalted butter
3 ounces unsweetened chocolate
3 eggs
3 tablespoons light corn syrup
2 teaspoons vanilla extract
1 cup whipping cream
Chocolate shavings for garnish (optional)

1. Preheat oven to 350°F. Mix crumbs, 1 tablespoon of the sugar, and the cinnamon together. Add melted butter and toss to coat. Press the crumbs evenly against the sides and bottom of a 9- or 10-inch pie pan. Chill.

2. Melt ½ cup butter with the unsweetened chocolate in the top of a double boiler over hot water. Remove from heat and cool to room temperature. Beat eggs, 1½ cups of the sugar, corn syrup, and 1 teaspoon of the vanilla together. Stir in melted chocolate and pour into chilled pie shell. Bake for 35 minutes, until the filling puffs up and forms a crisp, crackled crust. Cool on a rack, then refrigerate.

3. Whip cream with remaining tablespoon sugar and remaining teaspoon vanilla until soft peaks form. Spread over pie. Garnish top with chocolate shavings if desired. Refrigerate until serving time.

· · · · · · · ·

ORIENT EXPRESS

. . . .

Giant Chicken and Spinach Potstickers with Mint Dipping Sauce

Renata's Chinese Chicken Salad

Five-Spiced Barbecued Duck

Cucumber Ribbon Salad

Steamed Scallion Dumplings

Oriental Almond Cookies

. . . .

GIANT CHICKEN AND SPINACH POTSTICKERS WITH MINT DIPPING SAUCE

I make no claim for the authenticity of these potstickers, but I do know that they are the single most popular item at Indigo. We have made many thousands of these since we opened and have gone through some evolution along the way. I have always tried to serve items at the restaurant that people don't want to cook at home, and these potstickers are first on my list. To get them crisp, we make them in individual skillets over high flames, with fire, smoke, and fat sputtering all over the place—a perfect example of a recipe you just can't do at home. However, to the hoards who have requested it, here it is—without a cleanup crew. A more calming alternative is to make smaller potstickers, using only half an egg roll wrapper, cut diagonally, per potsticker, and deep-fry them until they're brown and crispy.

Makes 8, serving 4

½ 10-ounce package frozen chopped spinach
2 cloves garlic, peeled
1 ½-inch piece of fresh gingerroot, peeled
½ bunch scallions, 3 inches removed from the tops, washed well
Leaves from ½ bunch cilantro (about ¼ cup)

½ pound ground chicken
2 eggs
1 tablespoon soy sauce
1 teaspoon hot Chinese chili sauce
½ teaspoon salt
1½ teaspoons dark sesame oil
½ teaspoon grated lemon zest
8 (about ½ pound) egg roll wrappers

Cornstarch for dusting
½ cup Chinese plum sauce
¼ cup dry sherry
Vegetable oil for frying
Approximately 1 tablespoon sesame seeds

½ bunch scallions, slivered on the bias,
  for garnish
Cilantro sprigs for garnish
Mint Dipping Sauce (recipe follows)

1. Boil spinach as directed on package, drain, and rinse with cold water. Squeeze dry. Place in a large bowl.

2. In a food processor, combine garlic and ginger, processing until minced fine. Add scallions and cilantro and mince well. Combine with spinach. Add chicken, one of the eggs, soy sauce, chili sauce, salt, sesame oil, and lemon zest. Mix well. Fry a small amount in a skillet to check for proper seasoning, adding salt, soy sauce, or chili sauce to taste. It should be quite pungent since only a small amount is used in each potsticker.

3. Lay out one egg roll wrapper on a surface dusted with cornstarch. Paint borders with a beaten egg, place 1 heaped tablespoon filling in center, and fold diagonally; squeeze out air and seal edges. Repeat with remaining filling. Potstickers may be stored in the refrigerator overnight at this point.

5. In a small bowl, combine plum sauce with sherry. Blend well.

6. To cook, pour about 2 tablespoons vegetable oil into a medium-size skillet over high heat. Allow it to get hot, sprinkle in ½ teaspoon sesame seeds, and add two potstickers. Cook quickly on one side until lightly brown, flip, and break any air bubbles with a fork. Reduce heat slightly and continue cooking until lightly browned. Repeat with remaining potstickers. When all are cooked, dump oil from skillet, return potstickers to pan, add 2 tablespoons sherry sauce around potstickers, and swirl skillet around in circles over heat. Flip to coat other side with sauce and remove to a warm plate, sesame side up. Garnish with slivered scallions and cilantro sprigs and serve with Mint Dipping Sauce.

MINT DIPPING SAUCE
Makes about ¾ cup

⅓ cup fresh mint leaves
2 cloves garlic, peeled
¼ cup rice wine vinegar
¼ cup light corn syrup
1 tablespoon sugar

1 tablespoon soy sauce
1 tablespoon dark sesame oil
2 tablespoons water
Pinch of hot red pepper flakes

Combine all ingredients in blender except hot red pepper flakes. Blend, then stir in hot red pepper flakes. Allow to rest for 1 hour and serve at room temperature with potstickers.

· · · · · · · ·

RENATA'S CHINESE CHICKEN SALAD

Renata is an old friend who worked with me at Barbra Streisand's home. On occasion she'd prepare this meticulously minced Chinese chicken salad, full of crunchy celery, scallions, and special bean thread noodles. These noodles, known to the Chinese as *fen si*, puff up to a crisp when dropped in hot oil and are tossed with chicken strips, vegetables, and sweet and sour dressing to make this wonderful salad. Thank you, Renata.

Serves 4

2 whole boneless chicken breasts, skin removed
½ head celery, washed well
4 bunches scallions, washed well
½ cup hoisin sauce
1 tablespoon dark sesame oil
1 tablespoon peanut oil
2 teaspoons honey

2 tablespoons rice wine vinegar
1 teaspoon soy sauce
½ teaspoon freshly ground black pepper
Vegetable oil for frying
2 ounces Chinese bean threads (fen si)
2 tablespoons sesame seeds, lightly toasted

1. Cut chicken breasts into long slices, with the grain, about ¼ inch thick. Poach the chicken strips gently in lightly salted water until just cooked, 3–5 minutes. Remove from heat, add some ice to stop cooking, and allow chicken strips to cool in water for several minutes. Remove with a slotted spoon and set aside.

2. Meanwhile, cut celery stalks into 1-inch sections, flatten them, and slice lengthwise into ¼-inch julienne. Reserve in a large bowl. Repeat procedure to julienne scallions, discarding dark green tops. Combine with celery. You should have about 1 cup each of celery and scallions. Add chicken strips, toss, and chill.

3. Prepare dressing by combining hoisin sauce, sesame and peanut oils, honey, vinegar, soy sauce, and pepper in a small bowl with a wire whisk.

4. Heat 2 inches of vegetable oil in a deep saucepan. Heat until a bean thread puffs and floats immediately upon contact with the oil. Add the noodles in four batches, pushing them down into the oil for several seconds and turning them once when they rise to the surface of the oil. Drain each batch on paper towels. Set aside.

5. To serve salad, combine chicken and celery mixture with noodles, sesame seeds, and dressing to taste. Toss lightly and serve immediately.

· · · · · · · ·

FIVE-SPICE BARBECUED DUCK

A crispy-skinned, succulent duck, barbecued Chinese-style, is not all that easy to prepare at home, mostly due to the enormous amount of fat that must be rendered from the bird during cooking. I first prepared this duck on a rotisserie, which lends itself perfectly to duck cooking, slowly revolving for hours, melting the fat, and basting the bird as it turns. In Chinese households a more common practice for removing the duck fat is to steam it first in a bamboo steamer, allowing the moist heat to melt away the fat. Seasoning it and roasting in an oven allows the duck to take on flavor and the skin to become brown and crispy.

Serves 4–5

1 4½- to 5-pound duckling	1 tablespoon five-spice powder
4 star anise	1 tablespoon soy sauce
1 tablespoon minced garlic	2 tablespoons honey
1 1-inch piece of fresh gingerroot, peeled and minced	2 teaspoons salt
1 tablespoon peanut oil	½ teaspoon freshly ground black pepper
½ cup hoisin sauce	Cilantro sprigs for garnish (optional)

1. If the duck is frozen, thaw it overnight in refrigerator. Remove neck and giblets from cavity, saving liver for another use. Trim excess fat at base of tail and remove tail. Place star anise inside bird and hold legs together with a rubber band. Use a Chinese steamer or fashion your own with a metal steamer set in a pot of simmering water. Place the duck, breast up, in the steamer, cover, and steam for 1½ hours; check water periodically. Remove duck and allow to cool slightly; remove trussing. (Duck can be prepared in advance to this point.)

2. Meanwhile, prepare spice mixture by cooking garlic and ginger in peanut oil for a minute. Pour into a bowl and add hoisin sauce, five-spice powder, soy sauce, honey, salt, and pepper. Blend together with a whisk.

3. Preheat oven to 375°F. Drain juices from cavity of bird and remove rubber band. Spread marinade thoroughly over inside and outside of duck. Place on a rack and roast for about 35 minutes, until brown and crispy. Baste with additional sauce after 15 minutes. Allow to cool slightly, then cut the duck Chinese-style by removing legs and chopping through thigh bones, breasts, and back. Arrange on a platter and garnish with cilantro sprigs.

· · · · · · · ·

CUCUMBER RIBBON SALAD

This simple pickled cucumber salad has become a staple at Indigo. At the restaurant we use a special slicer that cuts the cucumbers into long ribbons. At home you can cut the cucumbers in just about any fashion.

Serves 4

2 hothouse cucumbers, washed
1 large red onion, peeled
1 cup rice wine vinegar
1 cup sugar
1 cup water
1 teaspoon sesame oil
1 teaspoon hot red pepper flakes
½ teaspoon salt

1. Using a vegetable slicer, cut cucumbers lengthwise into long ribbons as thin as you can. Or you may slice them very thin, on the bias, with a sharp knife. Place in a large bowl. Slice onion in half through root, then lay halves on one side and slice as thin as possible. Add to cucumbers.

2. Combine all remaining ingredients in a medium-size pot and heat until sugar dissolves. Pour over cucumbers and toss well. Allow to cool to room temperature, then refrigerate until chilled or overnight. Drain before serving.

. . . .

STEAMED SCALLION DUMPLINGS

Begin making these Chinese dumplings while the duck is steaming. Time your meal by shaping the dumplings about 30 minutes before the duck is finished roasting. The Chinese use some chopped barbecued pork in authentic dumplings, but I find the ham does just fine as a convenient substitute. You may omit the ham altogether if you'd like and sprinkle the dough before rolling with some toasted sesame seeds.

Makes 12 dumplings, serving 4

¾ cup warm (110°F) water
1 teaspoon active dry yeast
2¼ cups all-purpose flour
½ teaspoon salt
2 tablespoons sugar
2 tablespoons dark sesame oil
¼ cup minced baked ham
1 bunch scallions, trimmed and minced

1. Combine warm water and yeast in a small bowl. Set aside.

2. Using an electric mixer with a dough hook, combine flour, salt, and sugar. Add yeast mixture and knead for 5 minutes. (This may also be done by hand on a floured work surface.) Place dough in an oiled bowl, cover with plastic wrap, and allow to rise in a warm, draft-free place until doubled in size.

3. Roll out dough into a large rectangle on a floured surface, until about ¼ inch thick. Paint lightly with sesame oil. Sprinkle with ham and scallions. Roll rectangle into a long log. Using a sharp knife, slice it 1 inch thick. Turn slices on their sides and press the side of a chopstick firmly into the top of each, so the dumpling curls up over the stick. Slip the stick out.

4. Set a Chinese bamboo steamer over simmering water. Line the bottom of the steamer with a circle of parchment paper. Arrange the dumplings on the paper, leaving a ¼-inch space between them. Steam, covered, for about 20 minutes. Serve warm.

· · · · · · · ·

ORIENTAL ALMOND COOKIES

These and a bag of fortune cookies are a most traditional finale to a Chinese celebration. Lard lends noticeable extra tenderness to these authentic cookies that other shortenings just can't match, but those who must watch their cholesterol can substitute white vegetable shortening for the lard and four egg whites for the two whole eggs to prepare cholesterol-free cookies.

Makes about 40 cookies

1 cup sliced almonds
½ cup lard or vegetable shortening
¾ cup sugar
2 eggs
2 teaspoons almond extract
1¼ cups all-purpose flour
½ teaspoon baking soda
½ teaspoon salt

1. Preheat oven to 350°F. Grind half the almonds in a food processor until fine. Remove and set aside. Combine lard, sugar, one of the eggs, and almond extract in a food processor and run machine until mixture is smooth and fluffy.

2. Sift flour, baking soda, and salt together into a medium-size bowl. Stir the mixture in the food processor into the flour mixture with a wooden spoon until all ingredients are combined. Stir in ground almonds.

3. Place remaining almonds in a small bowl. Roll cookie dough into balls 1 inch in diameter. Press them on one side into the sliced almonds and place them on a nonstick baking sheet, almonds down. Flatten slightly. Beat the remaining egg and paint tops with beaten egg. Press one slice of almond in center of each. Bake for 12–15 minutes. Chill dough between batches. Cool cookies on rack.

. . . .

SPECIAL MOODS

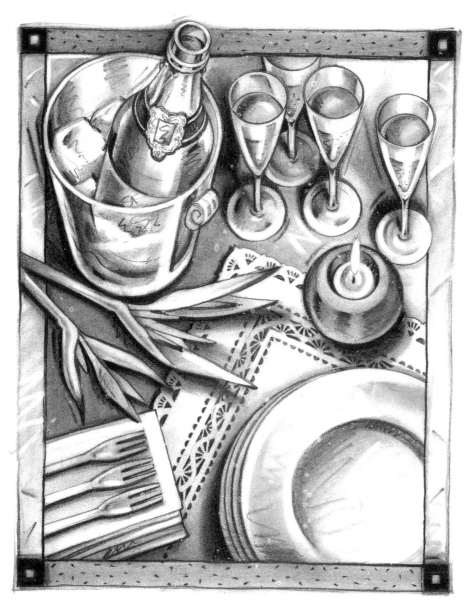

When an occasion calls for a particular feel or inspires us to cook for a special friend, we turn to the kitchen and follow our whim. The joys of our work satisfy the craving, as we savor the moment and toast the mood.

BUON ANNIVERSARIO

········

Shrimp and Arugula Salad with Shaved Mushrooms and Parmesan

*Chicken Bracioline Rolled with Spinach
and Fontina Cheese in Champagne Sauce*

New Potato Gratin with Golden Caviar

Jackie's Flourless Chocolate Cake

········

SHRIMP AND ARUGULA SALAD
WITH SHAVED MUSHROOMS AND PARMESAN

Common in Europe, arugula is now available in many American markets. It adds a great dimension to salads, and here it is combined with tender poached shrimp and slices of fresh mushrooms and Parmesan cheese.

Serves 4

1 tablespoon pickling spice	8 medium-size white mushrooms, cleaned
1 teaspoon salt	1 ¼-pound wedge Parmesan cheese
1 quart water	Balsamic Vinaigrette (see Index) or other
8 jumbo shrimp	vinaigrette
4 bunches arugula	

1. Simmer pickling spice and salt in water for 5 minutes. Meanwhile, peel shrimp, leaving tail flipper on. Butterfly them by making an incision along outside of tail and opening flat; rinse to remove sand. Poach shrimp in simmering water until just cooked, about 3–4 minutes; they are done when they become opaque, like a cooked egg white. Drain and refrigerate, covered with a wet paper towel.

2. Cut or tear arugula into pieces and wash well. Spin dry in a salad spinner and chill to crisp. Slice mushrooms as thin as you can and shave Parmesan by scraping a sharp knife across its surface, away from your hand.

3. In a large bowl, toss shrimp, arugula, sliced fresh mushrooms, and Parmesan shavings with a small drizzle of vinaigrette. Toss and add more dressing to taste. Serve on chilled plates.

········

CHICKEN BRACIOLINE ROLLED WITH SPINACH AND FONTINA CHEESE IN CHAMPAGNE SAUCE

The great marvel of this special dish is that it can be prepared before guests arrive, heated on cue, and served with ease.

Serves 4

2 10-ounce packages chopped frozen spinach
6 tablespoons extra-virgin olive oil
1 clove garlic, peeled and minced
2 tablespoons grated Parmesan cheese
Salt to taste
Freshly ground black pepper to taste

8 large boneless chicken breast halves
8 ⅛-inch-thick slices fontina cheese
All-purpose flour for dusting
3 cloves garlic, peeled and sliced thin
1½ cups champagne
1½ tablespoons chopped fresh dill, plus additional sprigs for garnish

1. Cook spinach according to package directions. Drain and squeeze dry. Heat 2 tablespoons of the olive oil in a large skillet, add minced garlic, and sauté for a moment, until beginning to color. Add spinach, sprinkle with Parmesan, salt, and pepper, and mix well over medium heat for about 3 minutes. Remove from heat and set aside.

2. Pound chicken breasts between sheets of plastic wrap until wide and thin. Be careful not to pound through meat, making holes. Arrange breasts flat, skin side down, on counter and sprinkle lightly with salt and pepper. Lay one piece of fontina on each breast. Divide spinach evenly among breasts and flatten to cover breast. Bring small end of breast over spinach and roll up. Secure with toothpicks. Roll each breast lightly in flour and set on a rack to air-dry.

3. Heat remaining ¼ cup olive oil in a large skillet and slowly panfry the breasts to brown evenly on all sides, about 10 minutes. Add garlic when the browning is almost complete; cook for a moment longer to lightly color garlic, then add champagne and chopped dill. Cover and simmer for 10 minutes.

4. When cooked, remove breasts to an ovenproof serving casserole; remove toothpicks. Season sauce with salt and pepper. Mash the garlic with a fork. Simmer sauce until it's the consistency of heavy cream. Pour through a coarse strainer over chicken. Garnish with additional dill sprigs. Cover with foil until serving time. Reheat in 400°F oven or microwave until bubbly. Serve two breast halves per person.

. . . .

NEW POTATO GRATIN WITH GOLDEN CAVIAR

This side dish can be prepared early in the day and then baked an hour before serving. The caviar you pass should be shiny and firm and not too salty. The eggs are far too delicate to be baked in the gratin, but they are a tasty and elegant enhancement as an accompaniment.

Serves 4

2 pounds small red potatoes, unpeeled
2 eggs
1½ cups heavy cream
¼ teaspoon salt or to taste
¼ teaspoon freshly ground black pepper
¼ teaspoon freshly grated nutmeg
1 tablespoon finely chopped fresh dill
2 tablespoons finely chopped Italian (flat-
  leaf) parsley
1 tablespoon unsalted butter, softened
1 cup (about ¼ pound) shredded Gruyère
  cheese
2 tablespoons grated Parmesan cheese
1 ounce golden caviar or more to taste

1. Preheat oven to 350°F. Scrub potatoes. Slice them thin and place in a pot of salted cold water. Bring to a boil over high heat. Cook for 1 minute and drain. Rinse with cold water. Dry well with paper towels.

2. Beat eggs and cream together lightly. Season with salt, pepper, and nutmeg. Stir in herbs.

3. Butter a 9″ × 13″ ovenproof casserole. Layer one-quarter of the potatoes on bottom of dish. Sprinkle with one-third of the Gruyère and one-third of the Parmesan. Repeat with remaining potatoes and cheeses, ending with a layer of potato. Pour egg mixture over top, adjusting potatoes with a fork as necessary so that egg is dispersed evenly among potatoes. Bake, uncovered, for 45 minutes or until potatoes are tender and cheese is browned. Let rest for 15 minutes before serving. Garnish with caviar.

· · · · · · · ·

JACKIE'S FLOURLESS CHOCOLATE CAKE

My old friend Jackie makes the finest flourless chocolate cake I know, and she must be graciously thanked for showing us how to prepare this joy. It's important that you bake this cake at the right temperature. If the oven is too hot, the surface has a tendency to puff, then crack. It's also very important to loosen the pan's sides immediately after removing it from the oven. Once cooled and wrapped in plastic wrap, the cake can be frozen for quite a long time.

Makes 1 10-inch cake, serving 12–16

½ pound semisweet chocolate
½ cup (¼ pound) unsalted butter, plus
   1 tablespoon for pan
5 eggs, separated
1 teaspoon vanilla extract
Pinch of salt
⅔ cup sugar
Powdered sugar for dusting

1. Preheat oven to 300°F. Melt chocolate and butter together in top of a double boiler. Allow to cool. Butter sides and bottom of a 10-inch cake pan, then line the bottom with a circle of parchment paper; butter parchment as well.

2. Whisk egg yolks and vanilla into chocolate mixture. Whip egg whites with a pinch of salt until soft peaks form; add sugar and continue to whip until they are firm and shiny. Do not overwhip.

3. Gently fold egg whites into chocolate mixture in three stages. Pour into prepared pan and bake until a toothpick inserted in the center comes out almost clean, about 1 hour.

4. When done, remove from oven and immediately loosen the sides with a knife, then invert onto a cardboard cake circle and allow to cool. It is normal for the center to sink inward. When cool, dust with powdered sugar and serve with a dollop of sweetened whipped cream.

· · · · · · · ·

A FORMAL AFFAIR

· · · · · · · ·

Chilled Lobster with Caviar Dressing

Bing Cherry Sorbet

Peppered Prime Rib of Beef with Garlic and Thyme

Horseradish and Scallion Cream

Buttermilk Biscuits

Chocolate Truffles

Lemon Pizzelle Cookies

· · · · · · · ·

CHILLED LOBSTER WITH CAVIAR DRESSING

Begin the celebration with an iced bottle of champagne, then proceed with this elegant appetizer. To alleviate extra work, you may purchase precooked lobster tails at any seafood emporium. If you don't want to fuss with lobsters, freshly cooked shrimp or crabmeat is an excellent substitution.

Serves 6

CAVIAR DRESSING
1 teaspoon water
2 egg yolks at room temperature
1 small canned anchovy fillet, rinsed with
  water
1 teaspoon dry sherry
1 teaspoon rice wine vinegar
¼ teaspoon salt or to taste
¼ teaspoon Dijon mustard
2 drops Tabasco sauce
½ teaspoon fresh lemon juice
¼ cup olive oil
1 ounce fine-quality black caviar

LEMON VINAIGRETTE
⅓ cup extra-virgin olive oil
1 clove garlic, peeled
½ shallot, peeled
1 teaspoon chopped fresh tarragon
Juice of 1 large lemon
½ teaspoon Dijon mustard
½ teaspoon sugar
¼ teaspoon salt
¼ teaspoon freshly ground black pepper

SALAD
1 pound assorted baby lettuces
3 Roma-style (plum) tomatoes, diced fine
1 1½-pound frozen lobster tail, cooked
 and chilled

1. To make Caviar Dressing, put all ingredients except oil and caviar in a small blender and puree. While blender is running on slowest speed, slowly drizzle in olive oil so a mayonnaise forms. Thin with water to attain a spoonable sauce. Remove to a bowl and gently stir in about 1 teaspoon caviar. Correct seasoning with salt and refrigerate.

2. To prepare Lemon Vinaigrette, put all ingredients in a small blender and process until smooth. Refrigerate until serving time. Wash salad greens, dry in a spinner, and refrigerate to crisp.

3. Prepare salad by tossing greens with vinaigrette. Arrange on plates along with a small pile of the diced tomato on the side; put some vinaigrette on it as well. Slice lobster meat and arrange in a circle over the tops of the salads. Spoon Caviar Dressing over the lobster, then, using the tip of a knife, garnish the lobster and dressing with remaining caviar.

· · · · · · · ·

BING CHERRY SORBET

Sorbets could not be simpler to make and are a refreshing interlude between courses of a meal. The intense scarlet color of Bing cherries and their natural tartness act perfectly in a romantic celebration. Make this sorbet the day before and transfer it from freezer to refrigerator when guests arrive so it will soften enough to be served.

Serves 6

1 cup water
2 cups sugar
4 cups frozen pitted Bing cherries, thawed
Juice of 2 lemons

1. Bring water and sugar to a boil. Boil for 10 minutes, then remove from heat. Puree cherries in a food processor. Add lemon juice and pour into a large bowl.

2. Mix everything together and freeze in an ice cream maker according to manufacturer's directions.

· · · · · · · ·

PEPPERED PRIME RIB OF BEEF WITH GARLIC AND THYME

If your romantic celebration is for a group of people, then this roasted rib of beef is a prime choice. If it's just you and a friend, you may opt to prepare your entrée as two individual steaks instead. Marinate them with the same seasonings given below and use your broiler or grill.

Serves 6

1 8- to 9-pound rib eye roast with bones
Olive oil
6 cloves garlic, peeled and crushed
Freshly ground black pepper to taste
3 sprigs fresh thyme
1 large onion, peeled and quartered
2 carrots, peeled and cut into large pieces
2 teaspoons salt or to taste
1 14-ounce can beef broth

1. Lay meat on a plate. Rub it with some olive oil and then the crushed garlic. Sprinkle it with pepper. Remove leaves from two sprigs of the thyme and sprinkle them on meat as well. In a high-sided roasting pan large enough to hold meat with

several inches of space around sides, place the roast, bones down and fat up. Pile onions and carrots around roast. Allow to marinate for 1 hour at room temperature.

2. To roast, preheat oven to 325°F. Sprinkle meat generously with salt on all sides and roast for 3½–4 hours, until meat thermometer reads 145°F for medium-rare when inserted in the center. Cook to about 155°F for medium-well. When finished, remove meat to a large plate and tent with foil. Allow to sit for at least 20 minutes.

3. Meanwhile, spoon off fat from drippings in roasting pan. Place pan on burner over high heat and sauté onions and carrots. Add beef broth to hot pan, reduce heat, and simmer for 5 minutes. Correct seasoning with salt and pepper. Strain and set aside.

4. To carve a standing rib roast, stand the roast on its side, with ribs to your left (if you're right-handed). Steady the meat with a fork and slice across meat, horizontally, toward bone. Space out your carving so that you will remove a bone with every other slice. Serve flat on the plate with hot sauce. Pass sauce as desired.

· · · · · · · ·

HORSERADISH AND SCALLION CREAM

Roast beef and horseradish make a good match. This cream is best when made in advance and simply pulled out of the refrigerator, whisked to lighten, and served.

Serves 6

¾ cup whipping cream
¼ cup mayonnaise
3 heaped teaspoons prepared horseradish
1 bunch scallions, white parts only, sliced
    very thin on bias
½ teaspoon salt or to taste
¼ teaspoon freshly ground white pepper

Whip cream in a small bowl until thick. Fold in remaining ingredients. Refrigerate until serving time.

· · · · · · · ·

BUTTERMILK BISCUITS

To achieve perfect biscuits, you must incorporate the butter and flour with a pastry blender or two knives. Knead the dough gently, about 12 times, to ensure tall, plump biscuits.

Makes 12

2 cups all-purpose flour
¼ teaspoon baking soda
3 teaspoons baking powder
½ teaspoon salt
⅓ cup vegetable shortening
¾ cup buttermilk

1. Preheat oven to 450°F. Place a large sifter in a bowl and sift together dry ingredients. Cut in vegetable shortening with pastry blender until mixture resembles coarse crumbs.

2. Make a well and add buttermilk. Stir quickly with a fork and form into a ball. Turn out on floured work surface and gently knead 12 times. Roll lightly until ½ inch thick, making sure dough never sticks to counter. Dip cutter in flour and cut by pushing straight down, without twisting. Arrange on baking sheet 1–2 inches apart. Refrigerate until ready to bake if necessary. Bake for 12–15 minutes and serve immediately.

· · · · · · · ·

CHOCOLATE TRUFFLES

After a large meal something as simple as a truffle is often the most welcome dessert. This basic recipe can serve as a base for your imagination; feel free to substitute pecans for hazelnuts, raspberry liqueur for rum, or anything else that meets your fancy.

Makes about 30

2 tablespoons unsalted butter, softened
1 egg yolk
¼ cup confectioners' sugar
¼ pound bittersweet chocolate, grated
1½ tablespoons dark rum
⅓ cup shelled hazelnuts, toasted, chopped
    fine, and cooled
Unsweetened cocoa powder for dusting

1. Cream the butter and blend in egg yolk. Gradually add confectioners' sugar, grated chocolate, rum, and hazelnuts. Mix well and firm in the refrigerator for a few minutes.

2. Shape into ½-inch balls and roll them in cocoa powder. Chill on wax paper for several hours before serving. Truffles may also be rolled in chopped nuts, coconut, or confectioners' sugar.

· · · · · · · ·

LEMON PIZZELLE COOKIES

These lemon- and anise-scented pizzelle cookies are thin, waferlike Italian specialties made individually with a special electric pizzelle iron. They are the perfect complement to fresh coffee at the end of your meal.

Makes 36

2¼ cups all-purpose flour
1 teaspoon baking powder
½ cup (¼ pound) unsalted butter,
   softened
¾ cup sugar
3 eggs
¾ teaspoon vanilla extract
½ teaspoon aniseed
½ teaspoon lemon extract

1. Sift flour with baking powder. Cream softened butter and sugar together in mixing bowl. When fluffy, add eggs, beating after each addition. Add vanilla, aniseed, and lemon extract. Fold in sifted flour in three stages, forming a soft dough.

2. Preheat pizzelle iron as directed by manufacturer. When ready, place a heaped tablespoon of dough in the center of the star and squeeze the lid closed. Hold squeezed for a minute to keep wafers thin. When lightly browned, remove and allow to cool. They keep well in a sealed container at room temperature.

· · · · · · · ·

SUNDAY BRUNCH

. . . .

Puffed Apple Pancakes with Pecan Bourbon Butter

Baked Eggs with Tomato and Gruyère

Swiss Chard and Leek Frittata

Gingerbread Griddle Cakes and Strawberry Butter

Golden Raisin Scones with Grandma's Crab Apple Jelly

Freshly Squeezed Orange Juice Gelatin

. . . .

This is a collection of Sunday morning brunches for a variety of moods. A simple raisin scone and cup of rich coffee is sometimes enough. Other times, hearty eggs or pancakes, or even a grilled cheese may be what you want, depending on your appetite and how much energy you can muster.

PUFFED APPLE PANCAKES WITH PECAN BOURBON BUTTER

A quick pancake batter is poured into a buttered sauté pan and then puffed in the oven, covered with spiced apple compote and Pecan Bourbon Butter. Both the compote and the pecan butter can be made well in advance, leaving just the pancake to prepare for your brunch.

Serves 3 (2 cups compote)

APPLE COMPOTE
¼ cup unsalted butter
3 small green apples, peeled, cored, and
    sliced ¼ inch thick
¾ cup sugar
Juice of ½ lemon
½ teaspoon ground cinnamon
¼ teaspoon freshly grated nutmeg
¼ teaspoon ground allspice
¼ cup raisins

PANCAKE
3 eggs at room temperature
½ cup milk
½ teaspoon salt
½ cup all-purpose flour
2 tablespoons unsalted butter

PECAN BOURBON BUTTER
½ cup (¼ pound) unsalted butter,
  softened
1 tablespoon shelled toasted, and finely
  chopped pecans
1 tablespoon bourbon

Confectioners' sugar for dusting

1. Prepare compote by melting butter in a large skillet. Add remaining compote ingredients and cook over medium-high heat until a syrup forms to coat the apples, 2–3 minutes. Remove from heat, pour into a jar, and allow to cool. Refrigerate until use.

2. Preheat oven to 450°F. Make pancake batter by beating together eggs, milk, salt, and flour with a wire whisk. In a large sauté pan, melt the butter until foamy. Add batter and cook until rim forms around pancake. Bake for 15 minutes.

3. Prepare Pecan Bourbon Butter in advance by whipping all ingredients together with a whisk.
    To serve, warm apple compote. When pancake is puffed and brown, remove from oven and dust rim with powdered sugar. Loosen sides and bottom with a spatula and remove to plate. Dot with Pecan Bourbon Butter, cut pancake into wedges, and serve at once with apple compote.

· · · · · · · ·

BAKED EGGS WITH TOMATO AND GRUYERE

Baked eggs are a far more common dish in Europe, and there's a great variety of ingredients that go into them. You can try all sorts of cheeses, sautéed vegetable combinations, and even sliced prosciutto. Be careful not to overcook the eggs; they will continue to bake even after you remove them from the oven.

Serves 2

2 very ripe Roma-style (plum) tomatoes,
   peeled, seeded, and diced very small
   (see Index)
1 teaspoon fresh thyme leaves *or*
   ½ teaspoon dried
¼ teaspoon salt or to taste
¼ teaspoon freshly ground black pepper
   or to taste
2 teaspoons extra-virgin olive oil
2 teaspoons unsalted butter
½ cup shredded Gruyère cheese
4 eggs

1. Preheat oven to 375°F. Mix tomatoes, thyme, salt, pepper, and olive oil in a small bowl. Lightly butter the bottom and sides of two 4- or 6-ounce ramekins. Place shredded cheese on bottoms of baking dishes. Crack two eggs into each dish. Arrange chopped tomato around yolks.

2. Place dishes in a pan and add enough hot water to come halfway up the sides of the ramekins. Bake just until eggs are almost set, about 10–15 minutes. Don't overcook the eggs. Serve hot with crispy toast.

· · · · · · · ·

SWISS CHARD AND LEEK FRITTATA

A frittata can be made with a great variety of cheeses, meats, and vegetables, putting no limit on your imagination. It differs from its French counterpart, the omelet, in that a perfectly prepared frittata is cooked very slowly in the skillet until the thick layer of eggs is set throughout.

Serves 4

1 bunch Swiss chard, approximately
  2 pounds
2 leeks
7 eggs
½ teaspoon salt
¼ teaspoon freshly ground black pepper
½ cup grated Parmesan cheese

6 fresh basil leaves, julienned
¼ cup olive oil
1 clove garlic, peeled and minced fine
3 tablespoons unsalted butter
¼ pound domestic (mild) provolone
  cheese or Swiss cheese, cut into ¼-inch
  cubes

1. Cut off the ends of Swiss chard. Remove center ribs if too thick and cut leaves in half vertically. Cut horizontally into ½-inch slices. Wash well. Cut off all of the green part of the leeks and discard. Make a slice lengthwise through each leek. Lay them flat, then slice lengthwise again. Now gather the leeks, turn them sideways, and julienne them into ¼-inch slices. Wash very well as they always contain sand. Drain in a colander.

2. In a large bowl, beat eggs lightly with salt, pepper, and Parmesan. Add basil.

3. Heat 2 tablespoons of the olive oil in a large skillet. Add leeks and garlic and sauté until limp, approximately 5–8 minutes. Add to egg mixture. Add remaining olive oil to skillet, heat, and add Swiss chard. Sauté over medium-high heat until wilted, another 6–8 minutes. Drain well and add to eggs.

4. Melt the butter in a large 10-inch sauté pan (with sloped sides, not straight) over medium-high heat. When melted, tip the pan to coat the bottom and sides. When butter sizzles, add egg mixture and turn heat down to low. Drop in cheese cubes and arrange vegetables evenly through the frittata. When the eggs are set throughout and only the top is runny, about 15 minutes, pass the skillet under the broiler for a minute or 2 to set the top. The top should not brown.

5. Loosen the sides with a rubber spatula and flip onto a large platter. Allow to sit for a moment, then cut into sections with a sharp knife and serve.

· · · · · · · ·

GINGERBREAD GRIDDLE CAKES AND STRAWBERRY BUTTER

Griddle cakes were always my favorite, and here, spiced up with ginger and cinnamon and topped with melted strawberry butter, they transform a winter morning into something wonderful.

Serves 4–6 (about 24 griddle cakes)

1 cup oat flour
½ cup all-purpose flour
1 tablespoon ground ginger
1 teaspoon ground cinnamon
½ teaspoon ground cloves
½ teaspoon salt
1 teaspoon baking soda
1½ cups buttermilk
2 eggs
¼ cup unsalted butter, melted
Approximately 3 tablespoons water
½ cup (¼ pound) unsalted butter,
    softened
¼ cup strawberry preserves

1. Sift the flours, ginger, ¾ teaspoon of the cinnamon, the cloves, salt, and baking soda into a bowl or 4-cup measuring cup. Beat buttermilk and eggs together. Add melted butter and pour into dry ingredients. Thin with up to 3 tablespoons water to desired batter consistency.

2. To prepare Strawberry Butter, whip together softened butter, preserves, and remaining cinnamon in a small bowl.

3. Heat an ungreased griddle over medium heat until a few drops of water sprinkled on the griddle bounce off. Drop 2 tablespoons of batter per pancake onto griddle. Cook over medium heat, turning as soon as the edges are dry and hold together. Cook until browned. Keep warm in the oven until all pancakes are cooked. Serve with a dab of Strawberry Butter.

. . . .

GOLDEN RAISIN SCONES WITH GRANDMA'S CRAB APPLE JELLY

There were always jars of crab apple jelly in my grandmother Til's cellar. During their season crab apples are small and tart and lend themselves perfectly to this pink, sparkling-clear apple jelly. Grandma used a jelly bag, which would allow the apple nectar to drip like maple syrup through the night. The jelly was "put up" the next morning, and we would enjoy it on everything throughout the year. The raisin scones are delicately sweet, finely textured biscuits and are best when still hot from the oven with a spoon of jelly.

Makes 12

1¾ cups all-purpose flour
2¼ teaspoons baking powder
1 tablespoon sugar plus additional for
   sprinkling
½ teaspoon salt
¼ cup cold unsalted butter, cut into slices
2 eggs
⅓ cup heavy cream
⅓ cup golden raisins

1. Preheat oven to 450°F. Put dry ingredients in a food processor and mix for a moment. Add butter slices and run machine until butter is cut to a coarse meal.

2. Separate one of the eggs. Reserve the white. Beat the egg yolk with the second egg and the cream. Pour into dry ingredients, processing just until all dry ingredients are wet. Remove to a board, flatten, and sprinkle with raisins; knead just to blend raisins. Roll out on a floured surface to the thickness of ¾ inch. Cut with a floured 2-inch biscuit cutter.

3. Beat the reserved egg white with a fork until frothy. Brush the egg white on the top of each scone and sprinkle with sugar. Bake for 10–15 minutes or until lightly browned. Serve hot.

GRANDMA'S CRAB APPLE JELLY

A jelly bag is certainly best for preparing homemade jellies, but you can substitute a big kitchen colander set on a saucepan. Line the colander with single sheet of cotton, cut from an old sheet. After you add the apples, tie it up with twine and suspend it over the saucepan overnight to collect the syrup. For the clearest jelly, do not squeeze the bag too much for extra juice. Just allow it to drip.

Makes 6 8-ounce jars

1. Gather about 4 pounds of crab apples. Wash them well. Cut them in half and remove any blossoms. Do not peel or remove stems and seeds.

2. Put the apples in a large kettle and add 3 cups cold water. Simmer, covered, until very soft, about 25 minutes. Stir frequently and mash apples with a wooden spoon. Pour the hot mush into a jelly bag and allow the mush to drip into a large bowl overnight at room temperature.

3. The next day, measure the juice and add an equal amount of sugar. You should get a good 4 cups, depending on the apples. Add the juice of a lemon. Bring to a boil and simmer to form the proper gel, skimming frequently. Begin testing for gel after 20 minutes. To test for gel, pour a spoonful onto a chilled plate and place in the freezer for a moment to hasten the gel. Check it after a minute; the jelly is cooked long enough when a skin begins to form on the top of the test and it forms a soft gel when moved with your fingertip; if it's runny, the jelly requires more cooking. Continue to test frequently so as to catch it at the perfect gel consistency. It takes about 25 minutes. (Note: If you cook too long, the jelly will be too firm and rubbery. However, if it's undercooked, you can let the filled glasses stand, unsealed, in a sunny window for a few days and the jelly will stiffen up a bit.)

4. Meanwhile, prepare jelly jars by scrubbing them and soaking in very hot water (or take them directly from the dishwasher). Pour crab apple jelly into jars. Spoon 1 tablespoon melted paraffin wax over each jar. When wax cools and hardens, repeat with another coat of wax. If you leave air holes, a mold will grow on jelly. Cover with lids when cool. A properly sealed jar can be kept at room temperature for a year.

· · · · · · · ·

FRESHLY SQUEEZED ORANGE JUICE GELATIN

This was something I first tried for Barbra Streisand, who loved fruit juices. She was so impressed with it that I found myself making all sorts of fruit juice gelatins—apple, grapefruit, strawberry, cranberry. This was her favorite.

Serves 4

> 1 quart freshly squeezed orange juice
>   (about 12–16 oranges) at room
>   temperature
> 2 envelopes unflavored gelatin
> fresh mint leaves for garnish

1. Pour ½ cup of the fruit juice into a small pot. Sprinkle gelatin over surface; do not stir. Wait for 5 minutes, then slowly heat the mixture until gelatin dissolves at about 110°F. Remove from heat and stir in remaining fruit juice. Pour into a glass 9″ × 13″ casserole and refrigerate until chilled or overnight.

2. Cut into 1-inch cubes with a butter knife before serving. Serve in chilled glasses garnished with mint. May also be made in a mold.

· · · · · · · ·

VEGETARIAN JOY

. . . .

Eggplant and Garlic Risotto

Parsley, Mint, and Bulgur Salad

Zucchini and Basil Fritters with Tomato Relish

Baby Artichokes Baked in Arborio Rice

Tuscan Barley and Bean Soup with Gremolata Pesto

Angel Hair Pasta with Slivered Garlic and Onions

. . . .

This collection of recipes is for those occasions when you'd rather not eat meat. They are all strictly vegetarian and can be served as side dishes or as one-dish meals.

EGGPLANT AND GARLIC RISOTTO

A risotto is a special way to prepare rice so that it takes on a naturally rich and creamy consistency. To achieve this, you must stir continuously while the rice is cooking. You may omit the ingredients that are animal products, depending on your personal diet. If you're not vegetarian, use chicken broth.

Serves 4

1 medium-size eggplant, peeled and cut into ½-inch cubes
5 cups Vegetable Broth (recipe follows)
3 Roma-style (plum) tomatoes, peeled and seeded (see Index)
1 bunch Italian (flat-leaf) parsley
2 teaspoons fresh thyme leaves *or* 1 teaspoon dried
½ bay leaf
3 tablespoons extra-virgin olive oil
1 small onion, peeled and chopped fine (about ⅓ cup)

8 cloves garlic, sliced fine lengthwise
½ cup water
1½ cups Arborio (short-grain) rice
Salt to taste
Freshly ground pepper to taste
2 tablespoons grated Parmesan cheese
1 tablespoon heavy cream
1 tablespoon unsalted butter
Additional grated Parmesan cheese or chopped parsley for garnish

1. Place eggplant in a colander and sprinkle with salt; allow to drain for 30 minutes. In a large saucepan, combine broth, tomatoes, half the parsley bundled together with a rubber band, the thyme, and bay leaf. Bring to a low simmer.

2. Heat olive oil in a large saucepan. Add onion and garlic and cook over medium-low heat until both are soft but not browned, about 6 minutes. Meanwhile, dry eggplant with paper towels. Add eggplant and water to onion; increase heat. Cover and cook until eggplant is beginning to soften, stirring occasionally, about 6 minutes. Remove cover and allow water to evaporate. Chop remaining parsley and add to eggplant. Add rice. Toss over medium-high heat for a minute.

3. Remove bay leaf from the broth. Add one ladle of broth to the rice and stir constantly until absorbed. When absorbed, add another ladle of broth. Continue, adding increasingly smaller amounts of broth until risotto is cooked al dente, approximately 25 minutes. Add salt and pepper to taste. Add Parmesan cheese, cream, and butter. Stir well and serve immediately on warm plates. Garnish with additional cheese or chopped parsley.

VEGETABLE BROTH
Makes about 2 quarts

½ cup dry white wine
2 onions, peeled and chopped
3 cloves garlic, peeled
2 leeks, split, washed, and chopped
4 carrots, chopped
1 zucchini, chopped
1 turnip, chopped
1 rutabaga, chopped
2 parsnips, chopped

3 Roma-style (plum) tomatoes, chopped
2 stalks celery chopped, with leaves
3 quarts cold water
Pinch of hot red pepper flakes
1 sprig fresh thyme *or* ½ teaspoon dried
1 teaspoon herbes de Provence
Salt to taste
Freshly ground black pepper to taste

1. Place wine in a 5-quart stockpot. Heat to boiling and add all vegetables. (Note: You may also add any leftover cooked or raw vegetables you have on hand.) Simmer for about 10 minutes, stirring occasionally.

2. Add cold water and remaining ingredients. Simmer, covered, for 2 hours. Strain through a fine strainer, pressing vegetables to release their juices. This broth keeps in the refrigerator for up to 4 days or can be frozen.

· · · · · · · ·

PARSLEY, MINT, AND BULGUR SALAD

This unique salad is called tabbouleh in the Middle East. It's prepared in many health-oriented restaurants but often contains too much bulgur for the amount of parsley. The key is to use ample parsley and mint to keep the salad fresh and light. Once the ingredients are meticulously chopped, it's quickly mixed, and you'll find that its freshness complements many foods. When piled on tossed salad greens, it can also serve as a low-calorie entrée salad.

Serves 4–6 (about 4 cups)

½ cup bulgur
¼ cup fresh lemon juice
4 firm ripe tomatoes, chopped very fine
1 red onion, peeled and diced very fine
2 teaspoons salt
½ teaspoon freshly ground black pepper
⅛ teaspoon ground cinnamon
4 bunches Italian (flat-leaf) parsley,
   washed well
½ bunch fresh mint, washed
½ cup extra-virgin olive oil
Lettuce leaves for serving

1. Place bulgur in a bowl. Add lemon juice, tomatoes, onion, salt, pepper, and cinnamon. Set aside.

2. Meanwhile, finely chop parsley and mint (you should have about 4 cups parsley and 1 cup mint). Add to bowl along with olive oil. Mix well and refrigerate for at least 1 hour. Adjust seasonings if necessary. Serve on lettuce leaves. Best if eaten the same day.

· · · · · · · ·

ZUCCHINI AND BASIL FRITTERS WITH TOMATO RELISH

These zucchini fritters make a wonderful appetizer. Large zucchini work best in this recipe since they contain less water than the smaller ones.

Makes about 18, serving 6

TOMATO RELISH
1 pound very ripe Roma-style (plum)
   tomatoes
¼ cup extra-virgin olive oil
2 cloves garlic, peeled and slivered
Salt to taste
Freshly ground pepper to taste
Pinch of sugar

ZUCCHINI FRITTERS
2 large zucchini
2 egg yolks
½ teaspoon salt or to taste
¼ teaspoon freshly grated nutmeg
¼ cup finely julienned fresh basil leaves
⅓ cup all-purpose flour
Freshly ground black pepper to taste
Vegetable oil for frying

Fresh basil leaves for garnish

1. To make the relish, core tomatoes and cut into medium dice. Reserve in a bowl. Heat olive oil in a skillet and add garlic. Cook slowly; when garlic begins to color, turn up heat, add tomatoes, and sauté quickly. Add salt, pepper, and sugar. Cover skillet and remove from heat.

2. For the fritters, shred zucchini and combine with remaining ingredients except oil; mix well. Heat ½ inch oil in large skillet over medium heat. When hot, drop small mounds, about 2 tablespoons each, into oil and fry until golden, about 2 minutes; flip and repeat. Meanwhile, reheat Tomato Relish. Drain fritters on paper towels. Arrange relish on plates and top with fritters. Garnish with a basil leaf.

• • • • • • • •

BABY ARTICHOKES BAKED IN ARBORIO RICE

My aunt Melina made this special creation for me in Italy one evening, and I'll never forget it. It bakes up into a unique one-dish meal and is sure to make an impression.

Serves 8

Juice of 1 lemon
16 equal-sized baby artichokes
½ cup (¼ pound) unsalted butter at room
   temperature
4 cloves garlic, peeled and minced
1 pound Arborio (short-grain) rice, rinsed
   twice
Leaves from ½ bunch Italian (flat-leaf)
   parsley (about ⅓ cup)
6 cups well-seasoned Vegetable Broth
   (see Index) or chicken broth
Salt to taste
Freshly ground black pepper to taste
3 tablespoons grated Parmesan cheese

1. Fill a large bowl with cold water and squeeze the lemon juice into it. Prepare artichokes by bending back and breaking off outer leaves until only the yellow inside leaves remain; don't be surprised if you have to remove more than you think, depending on the size and tenderness of the artichokes. Then cut about ½ inch off the top of the artichokes using a sharp knife and trim the bottoms flat. Place in lemon water to prevent discoloration as you work.

2. Preheat oven to 400°F. Rub the butter evenly on the bottom of a 13″ × 9″ × 4″ ovenproof casserole. Evenly sprinkle the garlic on the butter, then sprinkle with rice and parsley. Arrange the artichokes, stem side down, pressing them into the rice so they stand upright. Slowly pour in broth and sprinkle with salt, pepper, and Parmesan cheese. Cover with aluminum foil and bake for 45 minutes.

3. Remove foil and check to see if rice is cooked. If not, add water as necessary and continue to bake until rice is tender. Allow to rest, covered, for 10 minutes before serving.

· · · · · · · ·

199

TUSCAN BARLEY AND BEAN SOUP WITH GREMOLATA PESTO

For vegetarians the ham bone is optional, but to enjoy it as they do in Tuscany, use a smoked ham hock, remove the meat from the bone when it's tender, dice it, and return it to the soup. Serve it hot with a good bottle of Chianti and a loaf of crusty bread.

Makes 3 quarts, serving 8

1½ cups dried Great Northern beans
6 tablespoons extra-virgin olive oil
2 medium-size onions, peeled and chopped (about 2½-3 cups)
1 cup chopped celery, with some leaves
3 carrots, peeled and cut into slices on the bias (about 2 cups)
5 cloves garlic, peeled and chopped fine
⅓ cup chopped Italian (flat-leaf) parsley
1 small smoked ham hock (optional)
2 quarts water
6 tomatoes, peeled and seeded (see Index)
1 bay leaf

2 sprigs fresh thyme *or* 1½ teaspoons dried
2½ cups water
1 cup pearl barley
Salt to taste
Freshly ground black pepper to taste
Leaves from ½ bunch Italian (flat-leaf) parsley, chopped fine (about ⅓ cup)
1½ teaspoons grated lemon zest
2 small cloves garlic, peeled and minced fine
1 tablespoon unsalted butter, softened
1 tablespoon grated Parmesan cheese

1. Put beans in a bowl and cover with 2 inches of water. Cover with plastic wrap and soak overnight at room temperature. Or bring water and beans to a boil in a saucepan; remove from heat and let stand for 1 hour.

2. Heat 3 tablespoons of the olive oil in a soup pot over medium-high heat. Add onions, celery, carrots, finely chopped garlic, ⅓ cup chopped parsley, and ham hock. Toss for several minutes without browning the vegetables. Drain beans from water and add to soup pot, tossing to coat. Add 2 quarts cold water, tomato, bay leaf, and thyme. Bring to a simmer, cover, and cook gently for about 2 hours or until beans are tender. Add more water from time to time to maintain the level of liquid.

3. Meanwhile, in a separate pot, bring 2½ cups lightly salted water to a boil. Add barley, stir, and cover. Lower heat and cook until all the water has been absorbed and barley is tender, about 1 hour.

4. When beans are cooked, remove bay leaf, thyme sprig, and ham bone. Using a slotted spoon, remove 2 cups of the beans and vegetables to a food processor or blender. Process until almost pureed. Return it to the soup. Drain barley if necessary and add to soup. Continue to simmer for 30 minutes, adding water to maintain a creamy soup consistency. Add salt and black pepper to taste.

5. To make the gremolata pesto, combine the ⅓ cup chopped parsley, lemon zest, finely minced garlic, 2 tablespoons of the remaining olive oil, softened butter, and cheese in a small bowl. Stir into the soup the remaining tablespoon of olive oil and 2 tablespoons of the gremolata. Cook for 5 minutes more and serve. Spoon a fine line of the gremolata across the top of each serving.

· · · · · · · ·

ANGEL HAIR PASTA WITH SLIVERED GARLIC AND ONIONS

This dish takes as long to prepare as it does to boil the water. Cooking angel hair pasta is not a simple task, since it is very delicate and can easily be overcooked. If you're serving more than two, you may opt to change pastas, using one that can be handled more easily in quantity.

Serves 2

3 tablespoons extra-virgin olive oil
2 medium-size onions, peeled and sliced
  ¼ inch thick
2 cloves garlic, peeled and sliced thin
2 teaspoons fresh thyme leaves *or*
  1 teaspoon dried
1 bay leaf
½ teaspoon sugar

Salt to taste
Freshly ground black pepper to taste
Pinch of hot red pepper flakes (optional)
1 tablespoon unsalted butter
½ pound dried cappellini (angel hair) or
  other pasta shape
2 tablespoons grated Parmesan cheese or
  to taste

1. Put a large pot of salt water on to boil. Pour oil into a large skillet over medium heat. Add onions and sauté until they are beginning to color. Add garlic, thyme leaves, bay leaf, sugar, salt, pepper, and red pepper flakes. Sauté until onions and garlic are lightly browned and tender, about 5 minutes. Add a drizzle of water to keep them moist while cooking. Add butter.

2. When pasta water boils, cook angel hair until al dente, which takes only a few minutes. Drain in colander and add to onions. Over low heat, gently toss pasta around with onions, adding Parmesan cheese and more water as necessary to keep the pasta quite moist. Take care not to tangle noodles. Remove bay leaf and serve immediately. Pass a bowl of Parmesan.

· · · · · · · ·

INDEX

202